The Health Care Provider's Guide to Facing the Malpractice Deposition

Constance G. Uribe, M.D., F.A.C.S.

CRC Press
Boca Raton London New York Washington, D.C.

Library of Congress Cataloging-in-Publication Data

Uribe, Constance G.
    The health care provider's guide to facing the malpractice deposition / by
Constance G. Uribe.
        p.   cm.
    Includes bibliographical references and index.
    ISBN 0-8493-2059-3 (alk. paper)
    1. Medical personnel--Malpractice--United States. 2. Deposition-
-United States. I. Title.
KF8925.M3U75 1999
344.73'0411—dc21   99-40267
                                                                                        CIP

Visit the CRC Press Web site at www.crcpress.com

© 2000 by CRC Press LLC

No claim to original U.S. Government works
International Standard Book Number 0-8493-2059-3
Library of Congress Card Number 99-40267
Printed in the United States of America   5 6 7 8 9 0
Printed on acid-free paper

Dedication

To my mother, Modine Ashcraft Uribe,
who taught me that false accusations,
no matter how trivial, are ultimately harmful.

Foreword

On a scorching afternoon in June, 1990, seventeen hundred physicians and supporters marched in protest in front of the Arizona State Capitol Building. The heat of the day was easily ignored in view of the steaming anger and disgust fueled by a jury verdict and judgment rendered only days earlier. Dr. Abraham Kuruvilla, a neonatologist, was found liable for medical malpractice and the plaintiffs were awarded 28.7 million dollars! The monstrous size of the award only confirmed the legal chaos possible in a state where no tort reform exists. A relatively minor point of fact — the doctor had complied with the standard of care.

About the Author

Constance G. Uribe, M.D., is a general surgeon in private practice. A graduate of the University of Arizona College of Medicine, she completed her general surgery training at the University of California at San Francisco affiliated program in Fresno, California. It was during this time that she developed an interest in the world of medical malpractice litigation.

Dr. Uribe has been working with physicians for almost 20 years preparing them to meet plaintiffs' lawyers in malpractice depositions. Her seminar, "Surviving the Inquisition," was created to assist health care personnel in developing a realistic attitude toward the business of malpractice litigation as well as offer survival tips when confronted with a plaintiff's lawyer.

A strong physician advocate, Dr. Uribe has been active in political issues at the state and local levels and has served as Delegate to the Arizona Medical Association (ArMA). In 1997 she authored resolutions to examine the statutes for the Arizona State Board of Medical Examiners with emphasis on board member competency and due process, and in 1998 she developed resolutions for dealing with testimonial abuse in Arizona. She is an active staff member at Yuma Regional Medical Center and has held many positions on the medical staff. She authored the policies for dealing with peer review and impairment, wrote the plan for re-engineering the credentialing system, and created the Voluntary Investigative Leave of Absence for the hospital medical staff. She currently serves as Chairman of the YUMA IPA Credentials/Bylaws Committee and she developed the IPA Member Bill of Rights which assigns control of patient panel size, provider compliance, and provider discipline to the IPA and its members.

Dr. Uribe is a Fellow of the American College of Surgeons, an Affiliate Faculty for the Arizona Heart Association, a member of the American College of Physician Executives, and a consultant for the Greeley Company. She has also lectured at clinical conferences on breast cancer and co-wrote the book, *My Wife Has Breast Cancer and I Want to Talk About It.*

Acknowledgments

Putting a work like this together is similar to accepting an Academy Award — I don't want to ignore anyone who helped get this effort off the ground. I am reminded of a comment made by a famous actor, "If you think writing and directing is easy, just try it!" As a novice this was a formidable undertaking for me because I have always looked at the written word as a two-dimensional means of communication and I am a three-dimensional thinker. I find it much easier to face a group of people gathered for a seminar or prepare a future witness than to pick and choose which pieces of information will be successfully communicated by the cold, written word.

To accomplish my goal, I drew upon my own experiences and the experiences of so many others who have endured the slings and arrows of medical malpractice interrogation. Putting this all together required the assistance of personal injury lawyers, defense lawyers, judges, court reporters, and insurance claims representatives as well as the physicians I have worked with over the years.

Among those who made that extra effort to help with my task were Dr. Steve Wallace, Dan Jantsch, Duane Olson, Larry Cohen, Dr. Chaman Luthra, Scott Seamans, Dr. Humberto Rosado, Bill Bort, Paul McMurdie, Bob Roberson, Dr. William Masland, Dr. Stanley Pense, Scott Nett, and Dr. Joan Stratton. I am especially indebted to Leone Neegan, librarian at Yuma Regional Medical Center.

Not to be forgotten are the many participants from my seminars and the individual physicians I have coached over the years. Without their support and success my mission would be meaningless.

Mother always told me that when you are in need of friendship you find out if you have true friends. She was absolutely right and I must admit I have been blessed. Edna Harvey, Elaine Gerlach, Hellen Newland, Colleen Langewisch, Dr. Emilia Matos and Dr. Jerry Hamm endured endless jabber from me about this project and they listened like caring amigos. My longtime friend and maid of honor, Dr. Carole Browdy, offered her encouragement from the very beginning, and Shay Patterson was always willing to step down from Mr. Blackwell's list and add style to my life as did author and photographer Robert Herko.

As a young girl I was told that any man who married me would have to be very tolerant of my independent nature. Mr. Right took the form of

Richard W. Donato, my greatest supporter in this project. He was only made privy to the content of the book during the final drafting stage, but his patience while I spent long hours glued to the computer and his help in fending off the interruptions were invaluable. Rick is and always will be my knight in shining armor.

A special note of appreciation must be given to my new best friend, Dr. Abraham Kuruvilla. Not only does his ordeal epitomize the twilight-zone atmosphere surrounding malpractice litigation today, but his warmth and humor opened a new window for me into the world of life after lawsuits. Despite the bittersweet lemonade that resulted from the lemons given him, his courage and endurance should be a model for us all.

Table of Contents

Introduction

Litigation is the basic legal right which guarantees every corporation its decade in court.

David Porter

Reading this book will not protect anyone in the medical profession from malpractice litigation nor will it prevent pricey settlements and judgments. Its purpose is two-fold: 1) to introduce medical personnel to the culture of an alien civilization (law), and 2) to provide doctors and the non-physicians in our world a few options for dealing with our greatest nemesis — the plaintiff's attorney.

My quest for justice began years ago during my residency training in California. My program was blessed with visiting lawyers from major firms specializing in malpractice litigation. They would offer us tips on documentation and testimony. As a perennial student of human nature, my curiosity was piqued. I made it a point to study physicians, nurses, and other health care personnel as they embarked on their journeys through the creepy world of our legal system.

It didn't take long to realize that a large number of medical malpractice claims had little to do with medical negligence in the true sense. Carrying a *deep pocket* is tempting to a public that has access to pickpockets for hire.

There is no argument against a patient who becomes a plaintiff due to a mishap because of carelessness on the part of the caregiver, or a poor outcome as the result of care grossly deviant from that considered standard. Practitioners dancing to the beat of incompetence or imprudence should pay the plaintiff's piper.

Unfortunately, our society is filled with patients who are simply dissatisfied with their own care or the care rendered to a loved one. Many had expectations that were unrealistic to begin with and the best informed consent in history would not have brought them down to earth.

Several states require all malpractice complaints be taken before review panels where the litigation future of the cases depends on the panels' findings. Defendants in other states are not as fortunate, and complaints are taken *all the way* unless a process intervenes that leads to closure before trial. Such is the case in my home state, Arizona.

The Harvard Medical Practice Study III reviewed over 30,000 medical records from 1984 hospitalizations in the state of New York. Out of these came 47 malpractice complaints. Of the 280 patients who were identified as having adverse events caused by medical negligence only 8 filed claims, while the study estimates a statewide ratio of negligence to malpractice claims as 7.6 to 1.

Insurance representatives in Arizona report similar estimates: Only one out of every eight *victims* of malpractice ever files a complaint through the court system, and only one in 16 of all those filed ever lead to monetary compensation. Therefore, it is easy to draw the conclusion, as did the Harvard Study, that malpractice litigation fails to identify the true purveyors of substandard care and compensate the recipients of that care.

In the legal world, malpractice equates with negligence. The actual cause of mistakes and poor outcomes in the medical field may or may not reflect true negligence on the part of the health care providers. To err is human, but to be compensated for that error is every American's right in court. The law ideally cannot compensate based solely upon the occurrence of the error, but must show the error was committed as a breach of duty on the part of the care provider due to negligence that directly resulted in the outcome or injury suffered by the patient.

An anesthesiologist chipped a patient's tooth during a difficult intubation. He immediately contacted his insurance carrier who paid all the dental bills incurred by the patient as a result of the intubation. That is why we have liability insurance. Had the patient sued the doctor, a whole new world of accusations would have emerged using words such as *negligence, willful disregard,* and *deviation from the standard of care.* We know we live in an imperfect world, but it is the job of the plaintiffs' attorneys to convince juries that guarantees grow on trees.

The most important step in defending an unwarranted complaint is the deposition. This sometimes grueling ordeal is not only the first time the defendant has a chance to defend his actions or inactions, but it is also a tremendous opportunity to walk through the looking glass into a world where things are not the way they seem. The witness's performance during this deposition is carved in stone, so to speak, and will follow him or her around like a sword of Damocles throughout the remainder of the litigation.

This book contains a paucity of material related to The Law. I am not a lawyer. I am a student of human nature and that is the focus of this work. My concerns for my fellow caregivers are not whether or not legal processes have been followed or violated, as those are matters for the defense lawyers.

I have spent many years helping defendants alter their habitual logical and scientific approach to a more cautious, *out-of-the-box* way of thinking. After giving my Inquisition Seminars around the country, I am finally able to share the information with those who have not been able to attend.

Over the years the real challenge for me has been to help the health professional who believes that he has nothing to fear even though he has no background in deposition testimony from which to draw; especially the physician defendant taking the position, "Hey, I'm just going in there to answer questions." He might just as well start digging his hole and save himself the trouble later.

The book is written with the health care provider in mind and, therefore, some of the terms may be foreign to a lay person. The basic content, however, can be applied to anyone sitting across from a lawyer inquisitor. Also, I have taken the liberty of using few multiple pronouns (he, she, him, her, etc.) since I believe the masculine form in our language denotes a human being, not necessarily a male. I have never taken personal offense in finding the female gender ignored in documents, contracts, etc. Not having to deal with gender shifts also saves ink.

Many times the examples used from depositions are paraphrased to make them more readable. We rarely speak exactly as we write, and reading one's own deposition can be an eye-opener. We often find fault with our grammar, our use of certain terms, or the proper conjugation of our verbs. Frequent pauses are also annoying to read as well as repetitive remarks. Therefore, I have simplified the original entries into a form that demonstrates my purpose more effectively, and all names have been changed to protect the innocent.

A malpractice deposition is nothing to take lightly. As reported by Albert Clement Shannon, the power of this exercise was even known during the Spanish Inquisition:

> "All the evidence, the interrogations and the respons-
> es, were permanently recorded in writing, the names
> of the accusers and witnesses revealed, and the proofs
> opened for review."

From the standpoint of medical malpractice in our society today, we might rephrase the above to read:

> All of the evidence from the deposition, the questions
> and the responses, are permanently recorded in writ-
> ing, the names of the plaintiffs and witnesses revealed,
> and the documents opened for review.

Likewise, even the subject of closure or settlement was addressed during the Middle Ages:

> "In cases where the Inquisitor and the local bishop
> could not agree on an equitable sentence, the entire
> case was to be referred to Rome in accordance with
> regular ecclesiastical practice."

By our current processes of dealing with malpractice litigation:

In cases where the counsel for the plaintiff and the counsel for the defense cannot agree on an equitable settlement, the entire case will be referred to the court in accordance with legal statutes.

The similarities with the Spanish Inquisition do not end there. As John Elliott writes:

> "While burning and torture were in no sense the exclusive prerogative of the Spanish Inquisition, the tribunal did, on the other hand, possess certain distinctive features which made it particularly objectionable. There was, first, the secrecy and the interminable delay of its proceedings."

Anyone who has been through the ordeal of malpractice litigation is all too familiar with the instructions pertaining to silence about the case except with counsel. The statute of limitations for adults filing a complaint in Arizona is two years. Attorneys have a penchant for having the complaint served on the defendant at 4:55 on a Friday afternoon. That gives the defendant the entire weekend to smolder over the event and usually prevents contacting the malpractice insurance carrier until 9:00 a.m. the following Monday.

The case can go on for years. Lawyers, judges, and even defendants have been known to die (of natural causes) during the course of legal proceedings. The *interminable delays* in these cases serve no purpose other than allowing ample time for the lawyers on both sides to prepare for settlement or trial. Many defendants in the health care industry have *rolled over* into inappropriate settlements simply because they wanted it to end (see Chapter five, *Weighing the alternatives*).

Whether a malpractice case ends in settlement or at trial, depositions are the most important pieces of evidence. All of the facts elicited from all the depositions will play a major role in negotiations at the settlement table or in the courtroom. It is my sincere desire that each witness enter the deposition arena prepared to answer the questions as truthfully and accurately as possible, keeping in mind that any answer given may come back to haunt him by resulting in a bigger check to the plaintiff from his insurance company, or having his testimony presented to the jury as deceptive or contrived.

It is my intention to prevent medical personnel from becoming self-damaging witnesses and, as such, their own worst enemies. No matter what the outcome of a medical malpractice lawsuit, I pray that every health care provider will walk away from his deposition feeling confident that he told the truth with the best possible accuracy and without an aching desire to go back and change an incorrect answer. After all, nobody expects the Spanish Inquisition.

References

Brallier, J. M., *Lawyers and Other Reptiles*, Contemporary Books, 1992.

Elliott, J., *Imperial Spain, 1469-1716*, St. Martin's Press, 1964.

Localio, A. R., Lawthers, A. G., Brennan, T. A., Laird, N. M., Hebert, L. E., Peterson, L. M., Newhouse, J. P., Weiler, P. C., Hiatt, H. H., Relation between malpractice claims and adverse events due to negligence. Results of the Harvard Medical Practice Study III, *New England Journal of Medicine*, 25, 1991, 245.

Shannon, A. C., *The Medieval Inquisition*, Augustinian College Press, 1983.

chapter one

The law and legal thinking

> "Your spouses are going to change: their personalities are going to change in law school. They'll get more aggressive, more hostile, more precise, more impatient."
>
> *Soia Mentschikoff,*
> University of Chicago,
> to the spouses of first-year
> law students

They walk among us. Our society was invaded hundreds of years ago by aliens. They began as ordinary humans, but they voluntarily allowed their brains to be taken over by an unearthly power. Masters at concealing their reptilian personae, they are sometimes hard to spot. Their sexual appearances are rarely altered.

The males usually dress in drab pinstriped shirts with coordinated neckties, and the women share a similar conservative style. Consequently, they can blend in with any business-oriented profession. The cryptic comments out of their mouths may confuse and even alarm the unprepared. They are members of one of the oldest subspecies on our planet — *Homo sapiens jurisei*, attorneys-at-law.

Metamorphosis

The alteration in thinking and demeanor usually takes place during the first year of law school. I firmly believe that sometime during the second semester when it looks as if the student will not be a victim of attrition, an abduction takes place while he is asleep. The brain is removed through the top of the skull and twisted 180° and refitted to the cranium. When the student awakens, his perception is altered.

An interesting thing happens to a lawyer if he gets a judicial appointment. The new judge is sent to a training course. Again, during the night, the new trainee is abducted. This time the brain is lifted from the skull and twisted back 90° before it is returned to the cranial cavity. The effect is profound — the judge will still be unable to see things as clearly and simply as we do, but he will now be forced to look at both sides of an issue.

A colleague of mine, an anesthesiologist, is attending law school. During his second semester I asked him if he had been subjected to any brain-damaging rituals as yet. He replied, "Yeah, I think I have. My wife and I were on a cruise ship in the Caribbean when one of the passengers had an MI. He was being lifted from the ship into a water taxi and all I could think about was where a lawsuit would be filed if someone messed up."

This *brain damage* is what separates our professions. A prominent plaintiff's attorney, explaining how he lost a malpractice case for his client, said, "I blew it! I didn't do my job properly and we lost." At no time did he mention the possibility that maybe, just maybe, the doctor might have been innocent of any negligent act leading to injury to the patient. Lawyers want juries to believe the issues the way their clients perceive them to be, even if this requires forcing a square peg into a round hole.

A confusing trait of lawyers is their persistence in representing what we as onlookers may perceive to be a hopeless cause. Right up to the very end, the convicted killer with eye witnesses to the crime will have one, if not more, attorneys fighting for his life.

The drug-addicted mother who abandons her children will have a lawyer pulling out all the stops to convince the judge she has the attributes of a Sunday school teacher. Even in child custody cases, the legal eagles on both sides will point out the strengths of their clients and emphasize the weaknesses of the opposition.

The term *honest lawyer* may seem oxymoronic at first, but the legal profession upholds a firm obligation to the client. The lawyer is hired (on a contingency basis or otherwise) to represent his client's side of the story in a court of law. That is all he is supposed to do. He can't ask his criminal defendant client whether or not he actually did it — he can only listen to the client's position and present it to the judge or jury in a language they will understand.

The same holds true for the malpractice lawyers, plaintiff and defense. Even if he has a creeping doubt about the merits of proceeding with his role as the representative, counsel's job is not to be judge or jury but to paint a picture for the court that clearly shows the truth of the situation. In this respect, I suppose a lawyer can be viewed as a messenger. It's usually the messenger for the other side we want to shoot.

As one successful malpractice lawyer explained, "The truth is not what wins a case. It's convincing the jury to believe what you believe to be true." Before going to trial with a malpractice case, both sides will know what the witness' testimony will be, and the truth can be sculpted to make it easy for the court to come to the same conclusion.

A historical analogy

The ancient Greeks felt that the best way to ensure justice was to have a large group of citizens, sometimes numbering in the hundreds, hear the accused's side of the story and come to a conclusion of guilt or innocence. The responsibility was not placed on one man.

The Romans took this one step further. The Emperor could walk away from a bloody afternoon at the Coliseum with a clean conscience knowing the audience, not he, had decided the fate of the performers.

During the Middle Ages, the rule of the day was literally a trial by fire. The accused had to risk serious injury or death just to prove his innocence. Even then, there was no guarantee of vindication — those lucky enough to survive were often judged guilty anyway and put to death.

This is of more than historic interest to me. Our modern justice system has many things in common with those of our predecessors. For one thing, we use a group of citizens, usually lay people, whose job it is to give a "thumbs up" or "thumbs down" to the accused. We call them jurors, from *jurare* meaning *to take an oath.*

Back to the Middle Ages — The accused would have to put his hand in a pot of boiling oil to ascertain his innocence. Today's medical defendant is forced to hear accusations for every action imaginable, just short of putting a gun to the head of the plaintiff. (This idea frequently comes to the mind of the defendant at some point during the trial.)

Whether or not the burned hand healed with complications depended upon several factors. The hand was submersed in the oil for varying lengths of time with the outcome directly related to it, just as a defendant today will feel the intensity of the heat when the plaintiff's counsel spends hours and hours with opening and closing statements to the jury.

The temperature of the oil was important. We can easily equate this to the temperament of the judge and jury.

All things being equal, the underlying physical condition of the accused played a role in the healing of the burned hand. Today, defendants involved in malpractice litigation must have the inner substance necessary to deal with the pain during the trial, and to heal his wounds afterward.

A striking similarity

The practice of law is similar to medicine in that an attorney frequently chooses to specialize in a particular field. The members of these various specialties share certain personality characteristics. It has been my experience that the more humanoid creatures choose prosecution.

In many ways, career prosecutors are similar to primary care physicians in our managed care environment — their salaries are paid by a government agency, clients are "assigned" to them, and the goal is to protect society from undesirable organisms. Albeit, the organisms are of the two-legged variety, but they are damaging to our health just the same. From a personality standpoint, prosecutors think a lot like surgeons — they try to identify the problem and quickly eradicate it.

Attorneys who practice business law can be likened to internists. They are never in a rush. They can spend hours flipping through towers of paperwork, analyzing data and making suggestions for improving conditions. If their recommendations don't seem to work out the first time, they try a different approach.

Lawyers who deal mainly in personal injury and wrongful death have no recognizable counterpart in medicine. They live in a world of their own, specializing in turning people's misfortunes and sufferings into money. The reader may know a unique physician who fits this description, but no doctor in the history of modern medicine can come close to expending the amount of energy these litigators do, nor with the same tenacity. Working on a contingency basis fosters a level of microscopic probing and investigation that overshadows even the most complex of DNA studies we have available.

The moral paradox

Lawyers take cases to trial, not because they should but because they can. A case that reeks of profit will be tried to the fullest extent possible, knowing there is the risk of an unfavorable outcome for the plaintiff and money down the drain for the lawyer. Other litigators enjoy performing for a jury and a successful law firm with adequate financial security can try cases simply for fun.

On the other hand, a case that supports true negligence on the part of the caregiver may never make it to court or even bring in a sizable settlement. The actual condition of the plaintiff must be taken into consideration.

I assisted in saving the life of a 4-year-old girl at a hospital many years ago. She was not my patient. Two of the girl's physicians were sued and settled out of court. The other doctors caring for her were criticized by the expert witnesses in deposition, but they were never served with a complaint mainly because of a question about the existence of their liability coverage.

The lawyers representing the patient and her parents eventually added me to the list. Even though there was deposition testimony to support my heroic efforts, the Good Samaritan law does not apply in hospitals in Arizona and a settlement ensued.

Devastated by this decision, I asked my lawyer, "Just what am I supposed to do when I'm in a room and a patient arrests?" His answer was spontaneous. "Walk away. If it's not your patient, just walk away. That will be easier to defend."

It is difficult for individuals who enter the medical profession with the idea of helping people and saving lives to comprehend such advice. Why would we walk away? What trained professional in his right mind would turn his back on a 4-year-old girl in need? A hospital peer review committee would make mince meat of him.

The point my lawyer was trying to make is simple: A dead child is worth less than a living child needing a lifetime of care. A physician who negligently causes the death of an infant or child will be found less liable than one whose negligence results in damage that requires skilled care for the life of the patient. Also, a physician is not expected to have knowledge outside his realm of education and training and can walk away, claiming he cannot provide care that would be considered reasonable and ordinary (see Chapter three, *The standard of care*).

The majority of the free world learns that it is wrong to kill. Criminal law dictates more severe penalties when the victim is dead as opposed to injured. Personal injury law serves the client who has ongoing expenses, not loss of life.

The LMO — Legal Maintenance Organization

After going through the lengthy and expensive ordeals of friends' marriage dissolutions, I have come to the conclusion that the cost of a divorce in this country is directly proportional to the combined net worth of the litigants. Therefore, I propose a system of reimbursement for lawyers similar to the DRG-based method used by Medicare to compensate hospitals.

The lawyer would receive a set sum of money based upon the nature of the representation (CRG — Case-Related Group) provided, of course, the office staff coded the work properly. A bankruptcy, divorce, etc. would have set fees as would the various categories of criminal defense and other civil proceedings.

Just as with our coding system, there would be modifiers. The lawyer might need to add –69 for defending repeat sex offenders, or –86 for a complicated murder case, or a lengthy child custody matter might warrant the modifier –5050.

Those cases taking an inordinate amount of time would become outliers and would require investigation along the lines of our quality assurance and utilization management. Business associates, hired directly upon graduating from high school, would be given the NCLN (National Criteria for Legal Necessity), also known as the *Inkling List*, to give authorization for requested legal services.

This system would encourage the lawyer to not only expedite the process but to do so favorably for his client. After all, the key to success with this practice would be volume and the attorney would need to establish a good reputation to guarantee sufficient recidivism.

The Garden of Eden

The Arizona State Board of Medical Examiners routinely reviews all malpractice complaints filed in the various courts throughout the state. In 1995 alone, over 70% of the cases filed were found to warrant no further investigation from a clinical practice standpoint.

A phone call to the licensing board in Colorado revealed a similar estimate of complaints filed in that state were without clear-cut evidence of deviation from care standards. In California, as in many other states, it is customary for the licensing body to review only those cases which end in a verdict for the plaintiff or a settlement over a specified amount.

We can look at the defendant in a malpractice case as Adam in the Garden of Eden. Eve is the plaintiff and the snake represents her lawyer offering her a chance at the brass ring. There are few people who would deny anyone a fair day's wages for a fair day's work, yet lawyers attack a medical malpractice case as if it were the mother lode. Ironically, in some cases, it has been.

The plaintiff can walk away from a settlement or judgment with one-half to two-thirds of the kitty and, from that, the lawyer will subtract his costs. The plaintiff is frequently shocked to discover how much, or little, is left to take home — much like the devil's victim who finds he has sold his soul when it comes time to pay up.

As mentioned in an article from *The Arizona Attorney*, "Contingency fees are necessary...to prevent frivolous lawsuits." I mulled this over, trying to understand why an attorney would make such a remark since most licensing boards agree that the majority of malpractice complaints filed are, indeed, frivolous.

The key word here is *frivolous*. To a physician, this means *without justification*. To lawyers, it means *without promise of substantial monetary gain*.

The article goes on to explain how expensive chasing a physician for evidence can be. Obtaining a credible expert witness to testify against the defendant can run over $10,000, and this is money the attorney or his firm will usually advance the plaintiff.

During a lecture, a personal injury lawyer described visual aids costing over $15,000. He recommended to the other lawyers present that, while elaborate models were impressive to a jury, they should consider carefully just how much money they stood to pocket from the case before making such an investment.

Through the looking glass

Knowing your enemy is the best way to build a defense against him, and we usually turn to other members of the legal profession for assistance in dealing with the plaintiff's hired gun. The legal jargon alone can be overwhelming, so we need someone we can trust to take us step-by-step through the dungeon of malpractice litigation and protect us from the weapons thrown at us. It was shortly after I was served with my second malpractice complaint that I discovered how these weapons were not only unavoidable but predictable *and* sanctioned by my own attorney!

Two women sitting in the backseat of a car traveling from Texas to California were injured in an accident. I acquired them as patients while fulfilling my hospital staff obligation of surgical emergency room call. After operating on both, one woman died and the other survived. The driver cited for the accident hailed from Canada where tort reform severely limits any deep-pocket fishing expeditions, so the family, now living in California, sued the doctors in federal court.

The attorney assigned by my malpractice insurance carrier was very familiar to me since he had defended me in an earlier lawsuit. In the first case (another from an emergency call), I was dropped before the interrogatories were completed. During his initial visit to my office to discuss this latest complaint, he sat calmly across from my desk in his pinstriped shirt. Our conversation went something like this:

> ME: Mike, how long will it take to get me out of this?
>
> MIKE: Well, I've already filed an answer to the complaint. Then we'll go through the discovery phase and see exactly what evidence they have against you. There will be the interrogatories and I'm sure this will go to deposition.
>
> ME: What do you mean, deposition? I don't want to go to deposition. I didn't do anything wrong. I want out of it!

This conversation taught me to readjust my thinking. I could not approach this lawsuit the same way I approach my patients. Years later, I would understand the difference between our result-oriented profession and his process-oriented profession.

The world of medicine is result-oriented. If I see a young adult male with localized right lower quadrant pain, vomiting, guarding, and rebound, my thoughts are immediately directed toward removal of the offending appendix. I then take whatever steps are necessary to achieve that goal. An internist who sees a patient in diabetic ketoacidosis will act immediately to lower the blood sugar, and at the same time take steps to ensure the patient is adequately hydrated and electrolytes are in order. These steps will appear to be second-nature to the physician and nurses as the patient is returned to his premorbid state.

We approach ill or injured patients with an immediate goal — to make them well or, at least, more comfortable. We are constantly thinking ahead to the result of our treatment while working through whatever practice standards we have been taught. The desirable result is always defined, either consciously or subconsciously, right away.

Law, on the other hand, is process-oriented and, contrary to our popular belief, it is not carved in stone. Anyone who walks into a courtroom confident that the law is clearly on his side lives in a dreamworld. Our exposure to motion pictures and television may be partly to blame.

If laws took the form of the Ten Commandments, we would have no need for appellate courts. The *law* is not solid, but it's not liquid either. I like to think of it as *silly putty*. Any law that appears to be indisputable can be interpreted differently and redefined by a judge or jury at any time.

The Arizona Legislature recognizes that doctors are frequently reluctant to engage in peer review because it is not only time consuming, but their efforts go without compensation, and it is not the best way to win a popularity contest. Consequently, this unpleasant task must be given an "up" side. For the purposes of reducing morbidity and mortality and in the interest of improving patient care, the governing body of my state has a law protecting hospital peer review information from legal fishing expeditions (A.R.S. Sec. 36-445.01).

This law states that all proceedings, records and material, including all peer reviews of individual health care providers and the records of these reviews, shall be confidential and are not subject to discovery by the courts. This includes any discussions, exchanges and opinions found in peer review committee minutes as well as the names of participants present during those meetings. Consequently, peer review in Arizona hospitals would effectively terminate if we were suddenly subject to an unlimited discovery process.

In 1993 a superior court judge granted a plaintiff's lawyer access to the peer review data on the defendant physician from the defendant hospital. When word of this surfaced, peer review came to a dead stop. Despite the "law" that seemed clear-cut, the rules had suddenly changed, and this trend could have remained had the hospital lawyers accepted the ruling.

The Arizona State Court of Appeals in a special action, recognizing the statewide importance of such a decision, overturned the superior court judge. The Court also remarked that while the filing of a special action in cases involving discovery disputes is usually considered inappropriate, this request of the Court was justified because any appeal could not remedy the damage that might have been done had the hospital been compelled to supply the privileged information. After the ruling by the higher court, peer review business in our hospital went on as usual.

The final result of the malpractice complaint is floating out in space somewhere. The lawyers have to slow down and jump through a series of hoops in a certain order, dwelling on each hoop as they go. Each hoop is a process.

Attorneys think in terms of what the next process will be; Mike was thinking three or four processes ahead when he was telling me what to expect. As each process is completed, an opportunity may or may not arise to help vindicate the accused physician. Frequently, this vindication takes the form of a technicality. It's all taken one step at a time. The reader can imagine how frustrating this is for any doctor, especially a surgeon, who is familiar with cutting out the offender and putting it in a jar.

In the complaint mentioned above, Mike was able to get the case against me dismissed before interrogatories were written. This was due to a technicality concerning the way the case was filed and had nothing to do with my innocence of any wrongdoing.

A defendant in a malpractice case is foolish to believe that he will walk into the courtroom cloaked in truth, justice, and the American way. It's the American way, alright, but Superman is nowhere around. Any racing with speeding bullets, wrestling with locomotives, or leaping buildings will be done by the lawyer.

We pray that our malpractice liability carriers have contracted with law firms who have established reputations for being aggressive crusaders for their physician clientele. Unfortunately, a carrier may opt to give the cases to the lowest bidding attorneys. A defendant would be wise to check the track record of his assigned counsel prior to beginning any of the processes.

In either event, the lawyer's task will be to protect the doctor's *assets* with a vengeance. It is our defense counsel's goal to keep the monetary damages against us within the limits of our policy.

Defense lawyers assigned to a medical malpractice case will carefully review the evidence with their own consultants as well as outside specialists. When my own lawyer appeared in my office one afternoon and informed me that he was willing to defend me "all the way" in a malpractice suit, I merely looked at him and said, "Of course, you will. I didn't do anything wrong!"

Later, I realized my lawyer was actually telling me that his firm had reviewed the case, discussed it with other surgeons, and weighed the evidence as to the likelihood that a jury would reach a verdict less than or equal to my policy limits. He felt in his innermost soul that he could successfully protect my assets.

This difference in orientation frequently makes it difficult for a physician to understand all the processes involved in defending a lawsuit. It's not just a matter of being innocent — the defense counsel has to be able to convince the fact-finders (judge or jury) of that innocence. As one lawyer put it — persuading the jury to your viewpoint is more important than finding the truth.

The purpose of process orientation is best seen in the field of criminal law. The Office of the Arizona State Attorney General has a banner that measures 14 feet in length. It is a schematic showing over 175 legal steps and their possible interconnections. The shortest distance between the beginning and the end of the issue in question still involves more than 80 steps.

Even though it has nothing to do with medical malpractice, the patience needed to jump through each hoop is demonstrated by the banner showing the processes involved from the arrest of a suspect accused of first-degree murder until his execution.

An analogy close to home

Even in criminal cases, the hard-core question of guilt or innocence is not necessarily of prime importance. While home recovering from open-heart surgery, an obstetrician heard his doorbell ring and he saw a Hispanic man standing on the porch. Since the doctor was expecting a decorative iron work specialist to come that day, he did not hesitate to open the door.

The man asked, "Are you Ken?" The physician answered affirmatively. The man drew a gun and fired three shots at the doctor. The first went into his chest and he managed to dodge the other two.

The physician recovered from the physical injury and the young assailant was eventually apprehended. News coverage detailed the events leading up to the man's murder attempt after he confessed his two-year itch to see the doctor dead. The motive was culturally based — a male doctor had delivered his daughter, hence he had the opportunity to examine his wife. The healthy baby girl was two years old at the time her father tried to settle the score.

After deliberation, the jury found the accused guilty as charged. He went to prison, but on appeal was granted a new trial. The reasons were threefold: first, there was a question of whether or not the police had sufficient evidence to arrest him; second, the defendant was detained an inordinate amount of time prior to the actual arrest; and third, the manner in which the confession was obtained was considered unconstitutional. The appellate court questioned the processes leading up to his trial.

During the second trial, any information surrounding his original confession could not be presented as evidence. Also, it was interesting to see how the testimony of the witnesses for the prosecution changed from one trial to the next. Based upon the information presented to the jury, the defendant was found not guilty and was released.

A juror explained that there were so many questions left unanswered and the judge had made it clear that a decision had to be based only upon the evidence presented during that trial. The obstetrician was in tears when he heard the verdict. He relocated his family to another state, but as he explained, "It will never be over for us." The importance of the process outweighed the importance of the result.

References

Brallier, J. M., *Lawyers and Other Reptiles*, Contemporary Books, 1992.
When Justice Is Up To You, Association of Trial Lawyers of America, 1992.

chapter two

What lawyers think about us

"I don't know of any other industry, except the movie business, that has so many stars. Every lawyer thinks he's special."

Peter Morrison

The subject was doctors. "They hate us, you know," the lawyer sitting beside me whispered in my ear. "They *really* hate us." Not knowing my background, he assumed I was one of them. I wasn't sure whether or not to view it as an insult, so I wrote it off as a tribute to my talent for espionage.

"Perhaps they have a good reason," I proposed. "Naw, they get all bent out of shape when they're sued," he responded. "They take it all too personally."

He went on to tell me that he had been sued several years ago. He apparently had no relationship with the disgruntled client, but as a member of the law firm, his name was on the complaint. "Sure, I was nervous at first," he explained. "But then I discovered the firm had ample coverage and I didn't think about it anymore."

Interestingly enough, most law students do not have a clear idea how much professional litigators in this country are hated. Years ago I spoke with a physician who confessed that a plaintiff's counsel had angered him to the point where he actually considered hiring a hit man.

Lawyers often view us physicians and other medical personnel as unco-operative and undeserving of the courtesy they show us. After all, they dress up in expensive suits and appear very punctually at our doorstep with no other intention than to seek information, and how do we respond? We keep them waiting.

We may be counseling a patient in whom we've just diagnosed breast cancer or we may have squeezed in a child with an acute asthma attack. It doesn't matter. For whatever reason, lawyers perceive our dedication to our practice as deliberate avoidance.

I was never hesitant to speak to lawyers on any subject until several years ago when a situation fine-tuned my antennae.

Shortly after a malpractice suit against me had been dismissed, the hospital's lawyer asked to meet with me to gain information that would strengthen his support for the hospital. Anxious to help him with his defense, I arranged to meet him one afternoon in the hospital cafeteria.

I was only a few minutes late arriving. He began by asking the usual questions about my background. I did not feel this was pertinent to his case, but I answered willingly. Then he asked for specific details regarding my clinical management of the plaintiff, i.e., why didn't I perform a certain test, etc. After I figured out his true motive, I stood up from the table, and said, "I am willing to help the hospital any way I can, but if you think you're going to convince a jury that it was all *my* fault, you can get your support somewhere else." I walked away and never heard from him again.

It was clear the attorney wanted to shift the blame from the hospital to me (see Chapter nine, *The inquisition*). Despite the fact that the hospital personnel's treatment of these patients exceeded the standard of care, the insurance company settled for the amount of the hospital's deductible.

Lawyers still believe that physicians are only sued when they do something wrong. During a conversation many years ago, a young lawyer, Richard W. Donato, made a point of saying, "If a doctor gets sued, it's because he messed up. If money changes hands, that means he messed up really bad!" Angered by his remark, I wished for him a punishment so harsh that every day of his natural life he would be reminded of his arrogance. So I married him.

Three months after the honeymoon, I was presented with my first malpractice complaint. After a long list of doctors' names, it read "Constance G. Uribe, M.D., and John Doe Uribe." My husband was furious that the plaintiff's lawyer could not take the time to get his name right.

I immediately went to the Medical Records Department of the hospital to review the patient's chart since I did not recall the name. The patient was brought to the Emergency Room having been found in the desert suffering from severe heat exposure. He came in comatose, spent several weeks in the hospital, and was eventually discharged in his comatose state to a nursing home where he succumbed to pneumonia two years later.

I took a small part in his management by placing a tracheostomy to aid with pulmonary toilet. I could not remember caring for this patient although there was documentation of my procedure and conversations with the family. Some sleuthing on my part revealed that the family had been unsuccessful in getting any satisfaction from Workman's Compensation, so the physicians were being offered a chance to contribute monetary support to the survivors.

When the interrogatories arrived, my husband wanted to review them since he was experienced in these matters. From the back of our house I could hear his vocal reactions (they are not suitable for the content of this book). The first question read: "Doctor, state your net worth for every year for the past five years."

I was dismissed from the suit before we completed the interrogatories, but it was an enlightening experience for my husband and he took his crow medium-well with a little salt.

A few years later, Rick received a judicial appointment. Yes, he underwent further brain alignment. He quickly gained respect from both citizens and attorneys because of the fairness of his decisions as well as his demonstrated knowledge of the law.

It would be nice if we could learn the process-oriented way of thinking that a law school education provides (see Chapter one, *The law and legal thinking*), but we would have to risk the brain damage. An experience of my own taught me how naive lawyers actually perceive us physicians to be.

A group of Mexican nationals were arguing with U.S. Border Patrol agents when one alien came up from behind and was poised to strike an agent in the back of his head with a large rock. The agent heard the rustling, spun around and dropped to avoid the rock while at the same time, drawing his weapon and firing one shot into the would-be assailant's belly.

Twenty-three units of blood later, the patient was stabilized with his major vascular injuries repaired. A neurological deficit was discovered and prompted an immediate transfer to a tertiary center in Phoenix. I never received a follow-up report on his eventual outcome, so I was curious to speak with the two lawyers who showed up in my office one afternoon several months later.

The lawyers were informed that I would see them after I finished with my patients, since they had given me no warning of the visit. Since they had traveled from another city, they agreed to wait.

Midafternoon my husband (who was in private practice at the time) called asking about my schedule. When my receptionist mentioned the lawyers, he quickly suggested that I not speak with them. The lawyers called him back and the conversation went something like this:

> LAWYER: Why won't you let us talk to your wife?

> RICK: What do you want with her?

> LAWYER: We just want to ask her a few questions about the case.

> RICK: Have you filed suit against anyone yet?

> LAWYER: No.

> RICK: Then how do I know that you aren't making plans to sue my wife?

> LAWYER: (silence)

>   RICK: I think you'd better make up your mind whom
>   you are going to sue, then depose my wife and I guar-
>   antee she'll answer your questions.

The alien's lawyers filed suit against the U.S. Government. I was never deposed and I never heard about the patient again. These attorneys assumed, as many do, that I would cooperate in their quest to do a little investigation and not think ahead of the possible consequences. Relieved by my husband's timely intervention, I was alerted to a new *result* of what they perceived to be merely a *process*.

The legal profession has difficulty understanding why physicians take a complaint of medical malpractice so personally. The climate of managed care is conducive to destroying the time-honored doctor-patient relationship. Fortunately, many of us are in a position that still nurtures trust between us and our "clients," as they are called today. Most of us know how important this relationship can be. Patients get well faster and are more comfortable when they have confidence in their caregivers.

That care we give affects people's lives forever. The public may or may not remember the name of a lawyer, but we can rest assured they can run off the name of every surgeon who operated on them no matter how long ago. It's like having squatter's rights — we make changes that improve patients' conditions and, therefore, are entitled to a certain amount of own-ership. This bond that develops is the main force driving physicians to make the personal sacrifices necessary to practice medicine in an atmosphere of unlimited availability.

I was chatting with a colleague, a family practitioner. He was disillu-sioned over the way managed care was coming between him and his patients. He explained, "I went into medicine to take care of people and their families, to establish a life-long relationship. Now I have patients picking up their records because they changed insurance companies and I'm not on the list."

"Then I'll inherit a new patient with a million problems, and he's been followed for years by another doctor who is very familiar with him, and he doesn't seem at all bothered by the change. It's not fair to us or to the patients." This physician was also aware of the value of that close relation-ship when dealing with the patient who has experienced an unexpected or undesirable outcome.

Physicians have worked hard over the past two hundred years to develop a reputation for integrity and competence. Being accused of harming a patient or not living up to the patient's expectations can be a blow that knocks the breath right out of us. A doctor cares for a patient with his heart open, then that patient reciprocates by ripping it out. There may or may not be any truth to the accusations, but the claim alone can damage the doctor's reputation, cause severe depression, and upset his entire family. Yes, we do take it personally, and I pray we always will.

Another concept that confuses lawyers is our relationships with each other, but the managed care environment has affected that as well. The convenience of readily available health care for doctors, nurses, and their families is slowly dribbling off the court. The legal profession does not understand how medical people can be so willing to take such an active part in caring for each other and, in many instances, that care has been given with little concern of payment for services rendered. Donating this type of *pro bono* care along with other charity work may appear peculiar and unorthodox to a profession in which such behavior has to be declared mandatory or is strongly suggested by the rules from a higher court.

Lawyers tend to focus on the malpractice aspect of our profession without giving relevance to the concept of "best intentions" or "will of God." While we have complained over the past three decades about the "crisis" in the area of malpractice litigation, our legal opponents have an alternative, albeit biased, solution to the problem.

It is their opinion that medical malpractice litigation will disappear when physicians are more severely punished for their actions. The fact that only a small percentage of doctors in this country are disciplined each year by censure, restriction of privileges, suspension or revocation of license speaks for itself. There are still over half a million of us loose and roaming the streets with licenses to harm the unsuspecting public. Lawyers contend we simply do not police ourselves closely enough nor do we deal with the deviate doctors appropriately.

In fact, physicians, after being dismissed from malpractice complaints, are able to avoid appearance in the National Practitioner Data Bank (see Chapter five, *Weighing the alternatives*). Lawyers would prefer to see all defendants listed somewhere. It is their contention that avoiding Data Bank recognition does not equate with absolute adherence to the standard of care.

Despite the attitude most malpractice attorneys share that we are guilty until proven innocent, they maintain that we overestimate our risk of liability. This is based on the assumption that only a small percentage of cases lead to a major judgment for the plaintiff, and the majority of those result in judgments far less than the defendant's insurance policy limits. On the other hand, physician defendants measure liability risk in terms of the effect it has on their families, their practices, their physical and mental health, and their assets, as well as the possibility of a star on the National Practitioner Data Bank walk of fame.

Awareness of the legal world's attitudes toward us does not afford any assurance that the totally binding no-fault bad-things-happen-to-good-patients remediation light can be seen at the end of the malpractice litigation tunnel. As long as lawyers feel that the contents of medicine's deep pockets should be donated to support the consequences of their clients' misfortunes, personal injury law will thrive. With that in mind, we must focus on dealing with the problem at hand, learning as much as we can about our nemesis, and being ready if and when an actual confrontation occurs. When we see the jousting pole heading our way is not the time to think about donning the armour.

Reference

Brallier, J. M., *Lawyers and Other Reptiles*, Contemporary Books, 1992.

chapter three

The standard of care

> "...though the will of the majority is in all cases to
> prevail, that will, to be rightful, must be reasonable..."
>
> *Thomas Jefferson*

About 20 years ago, I was sitting on a plane next to a distinguished middle-aged gentleman. When he finished with the morning paper, he asked my opinion about the headline — another palimony suit had made the news. After discussing the pros and cons of cohabitation, the man explained that he was a lawyer who had recently been victorious in a palimony case.

I congratulated him on his success and he confessed that his true love was medical malpractice. In fact, at that moment he was en route to a deposition. "Fascinating," I quipped with a smile. The lawyer went on to explain generalities of the case, using terms of two syllables or less when criticizing the defendant physicians. I held onto his every word.

Puffed up and ready to avenge injustice in the medical arena, he finally asked, "So, tell me, are you a working girl?" I was in my surgical residency at the time, and I did not miss the opportunity to inform the suited crusader of his distorted perception of the standard of care in the case he was on his way to try.

Somewhat deflated, he sat back in his seat and sighed, "I knew this would happen to me someday." When we landed, the lawyer anxiously carried my luggage to the taxi. "I don't have a good feeling about this anymore," he said.

A jury of our peers

A mock trial was presented several years ago at an American College of Surgeons meeting in Phoenix. I eagerly watched as the plaintiff's counsel, defendant, defense counsel, and defendant's expert witness performed a one-act play with a real-life judge present. The audience was the jury.

I could tell by the whispers throughout that most of my colleagues were leaning toward a plaintiff's verdict. After asking permission to speak, I stood up and gave a 30-second definition of the standard of care. The group turned *en masse* toward the judge, silently looking for his reaction to my comment. The judge stared at the ceiling for a moment and said, "What do you want me to say? She's absolutely right." The atmosphere surrounding the trial suddenly took on a different light.

A jury of medical people judging medical people has a downside. It is entirely possible that a group of our true peers would hold us to a much higher standard than men off the street. Our own professional expectations differ from those of the public. What is routine for a specialist in a large, tertiary care center may be difficult for the same specialist practicing in a rural community with limited facilities. What is reasonable and ordinary might be a concept difficult for the tertiary center specialist to grasp.

It is easy for practitioners to criticize each other during peer review or quality assurance meetings. Even with documented informed consent, our profession has a tendency to examine a colleague's actions with a level of knowledge far beyond that required by law. Our medical hindsight is infallible and can easily cloud common reason. It is important that we understand the standard of care as defined in a court of law and judge a health care provider in a malpractice complaint accordingly.

To err is human, to forgive takes litigation

Many years ago, attorneys representing a hospital responded to a request from a plaintiff's lawyer — over 80 charts were handed over for that lawyer's examination. Since none of those charts were related in any way to the case in litigation and they contained the names of dozens of other physicians as well as the defendant, the medical staff at the hospital was infuriated.

Special counsel was hired by the staff to explain avenues of recourse at this point. It was known by the physicians present that the hospital attorneys could be subjected to state and federal fines for divulging this confidential information. The lawyer's explanation was simple, "Hey, they made a mistake, okay? People make mistakes."

What happens if a doctor or nurse makes a mistake? Perhaps nothing. Perhaps something devastating. Medication errors are known to happen in the best of circumstances, yet does that constitute negligence?

I recall one of my junior residents having to place a central venous catheter in a patient very quickly. He had a nurse at the bedside assisting him. She held up a bottle from which the resident withdrew a few cc's of Lidocaine to anesthetize the skin. The nurse noticed an error as soon as the local anesthetic had been infiltrated — she had mistakenly grabbed a bottle of Norepinephrine. The resident handled the error appropriately and there were no adverse sequelae.

Were the doctor and/or nurse negligent? Was the medication misplaced with the intent of harming a patient? Was there willful disregard for this critical patient's well-being? Probably not. The doctor was trying to get the urgent line in the patient, glanced at the bottle, noticed the white and blue label, and assumed it was the proper drug. Most of us are in the habit of examining the bottle more carefully before drawing a medication, but this error occurred, was recognized immediately, and steps were taken to rectify the problem.

Medicine is a team effort. A relatively simple procedure such as placing a central line requires the involvement of dozens of human beings — the doctor, the nurse, the pharmacists, the drug manufacturers, the central supply employees, the manufacturers of the catheters, the suppliers of the IV solutions, and the list goes on. If we could not rely on each link in the chain, we could not practice our craft.

Personal injury lawyers drool over little breaks in the chains. Any mishap, whether truly negligent or otherwise, will be milked to its fullest. Simply stated: Mistakes in medicine, unlike mistakes in law, are simply not tolerated. Errors should never occur and, if they do, someone has to pay.

Plaintiff lawyers will also try to squelch any evidence of their clients' own involvement in their misfortunes. A lawyer managed to keep from a jury information related to a patient's lengthy smoking history during a trial against a physician accused of negligence in managing his end-staged lung disease.

The purpose of medical malpractice litigation is to convince a jury that it was all the defendant's fault. Death or injury would not have occurred had it not been for the actions or inactions of the defendant. The patient's actions or inactions are never held to standards that would be considered *reasonable and ordinary*.

The common denominator of care

When comparing one physician's management with another's, the issue of Standard of Care (SOC) always arises. It is important to understand that lack of sophisticated clinical wisdom does not, in itself, equate with medical negligence. When we question actions or inactions during a quality assurance review, we are holding the physicians to a much higher standard than do our courts of law.

To answer the questions about SOC accurately, we must examine how the court views the physician's role in providing health care. We will see how this can apply to all caregivers — physicians, nurses, paramedics, and other practitioners.

The Standard of Care concept was established over a hundred years ago. Medical malpractice in the United States came into being in the mid-1800s before the Civil War. Prior to the turn of the century, the courts were forced to define a principle that, fortunately, has survived these many years.

If a physician offered care to a patient, it was implied that he possessed a *reasonable* degree of learning and skill, the same as that possessed by other physicians in his locality. It was that physician's duty to use *reasonable* care and diligence in his treatment of the patient. He was *not* required to possess extraordinary learning or skill that could only belong to a rare few. He was only expected to have the learning and skills of an *average* practitioner. Therefore, to find a physician liable, the plaintiff had to prove that the lack of *reasonable* and *ordinary* care led to a bad result.

Originally, the definition was used to identify a *community* standard; but as training programs became similar in teaching and experience, the idea was broadened to define a *national* standard. Today, a brain surgeon's management of a patient in Winslow will be compared to that of a brain surgeon in Fresno or Nashville.

At one time there was a basis for distinguishing between rural and metropolitan areas, but that sort of variation is rarely considered today unless a community simply does not possess certain equipment or transfer capabilities. A patient with an acute bleed from an intracranial aneurysm is expected to undergo evaluation at the hands of a neurosurgeon as soon as possible. If that patient initially presents to a small, rural hospital, the SOC is still the same — get the patient to a neurosurgeon as soon as possible, even if it involves transport.

The court still speaks of a SOC that is *reasonable* and *ordinary*. In other words, how does the defendant's care compare to that of a similarly trained physician elsewhere in this country? We must ask ourselves to define the actual *common denominator* of the management. By that I mean we have to find what specifics of the care would be common to other physicians given the same patient. This does not apply to the world's greatest specialist in this particular field or the researcher who has just developed a new treatment. Whatever this common denominator, it should be lacking in the defendant for the court to prove that the physician was at fault.

If we were able to take all the actions pertaining to management of a particular disease or procedure and put them in a large sieve, we could imagine all of the "loner" actions falling through the holes. The larger, more common actions would remain behind. The retained contents would constitute the standard of care.

As an exercise, we'll pretend Dr. A is served with a complaint that he was negligent in diagnosing a breast cancer in a patient. Upon review of Dr. A's records, we find that he saw the patient once. She presented with a tender area in her right breast and a normal mammogram report. Dr. A documented a non-discrete area of thickening that was very tender. He recommended she avoid all caffeine products, take Vitamin E, and return for another exam in one month. He never saw her again. She presented six months later to another physician who diagnosed the malignancy.

The plaintiff finds an expert witness to testify that a fine needle aspiration of the thickened area should have been performed at the initial visit. To find the common denominator of care, we consult three other physicians who have equivalent education and training as Dr. A. Each is presented with the same case, but without the known outcome. We then record the comments:

Dr. B: I would probably plug the woman's history into my database and determine what her risk is for developing breast cancer and base my follow-up on that.

Dr. C: I would order an ultrasound with or without aspiration of any underlying cystic structures and follow-up would depend on that.

Dr. D: I would order an ultrasound and possibly a Miraluma™ scan and see the patient again.

If we carefully sift through each of the above responses, we will find a *common denominator*: follow-up. Then we ask, did Dr. A have any plans for follow-up? Since the answer is affirmative, we can conclude that Dr. A upheld the standard of care.

An expert witness reviewing a case for a malpractice lawyer should keep in mind the common denominator of care. It is always easy to criticize a colleague given the outcome and all the documentation leading up to it. An expert should begin such a review by reading the original office or admission notes, not the discharge summary. The potential witness should make note of any and all actions that appear appropriate based upon the information documented in the order in which the details of the case unfold.

Those actions listed will constitute the SOC for that particular case. Any thoughts the witness may have regarding other actions which could be deemed appropriate given the same circumstances along with actions appearing unnecessary or questionable should be listed in a different column. Those notations may become important in supporting the plaintiff's position.

On the other hand, if our potential expert witness is given the plaintiff's bias in the beginning, he should take a blank sheet of paper and list what he believes to be the minimum standards which should be met prior to his examining the documentation. He can then check off each action as it presents itself in the record.

A physician had mixed feelings when asked by a plaintiff's lawyer to review a record. The doctor wanted to tell the lawyer he had no cause of action against the treating specialist, but as he explained, "I was told in training never to do what this doctor did."

My question to him was, "Are there doctors who would consider this action as keeping within the standard of care?" "Oh, yeah, I just read an article mentioning this," he replied. In that case, the action fell under the *respectable minority* category.

Even though this particular reviewer and, possibly, the majority of specialists would not act in this way, there is a *respectable minority* of physicians who would. That discovery allowed the potential expert witness to present his opinion to the plaintiff's lawyer keeping the focus on what is reasonable and ordinary.

To borrow a method pioneered by Walt Disney, a potential witness can review a case by initially jotting down everything that is right with the management, all the actions he immediately approves. Then the witness should asked himself, "What is missing? What appears to be wrong?" Again, the reviewer should decide whether or not any action or inaction grossly deviates from standard management or could be held as acceptable by a respectable minority.

During a deposition there will always be questions concerning the SOC. When these arise, it is important for the witness to concentrate and come up with a common denominator in his mind.

From one of my own depositions, I offer the following:

> LAWYER: Would you agree with me that if six to eight minutes of cardiac arrest went by before the Epinephrine was given, it violated the standard of care for a resuscitation at Anytown Hospital on March 10th, 1984?
>
> WITNESS: No, I can't agree with that.
>
> LAWYER: Why, Ma'am?

I knew the lawyer was getting upset with me here because he called me *Ma'am*. I sat back for a moment and thought about his hypothetical question. I asked myself, "If a patient has a cardiac arrest in any hospital, what would be the expected action of the people arriving at the scene." I had to decide what would be going on during the first six minutes no matter where the arrest occurred. I then identified the common denominator — CPR.

> WITNESS: If nothing is being done and six to eight minutes pass, that's a deviation in the standard of care. If the patient is undergoing CPR, that is the standard of care in an arrest situation.

One easy trap physicians must avoid during a deposition is the tendency to establish standards in a field other than their own. A plaintiff's lawyers will frequently ask about another doctor's or nurse's management to establish a SOC. The following example illustrates a common form of questioning:

> LAWYER: If Dr. Jones wasn't sure that his anesthesia equipment was operating properly or that his circuits were intact, would he not disconnect the patient from the equipment entirely and manually bag?
>
> WITNESS: I do not know what the standard of care would be for anesthesiologists in that situation.

If the witness had fallen into this trap, the lawyer could have used the answer against another physician despite any testimony to the contrary by members of that specialty. This witness has made it a practice to study SOCs for surgeons and leave the other fields to those more qualified. Unfortunately, courts of law do not have rigid criteria for qualifying witnesses to testify to the standards of care (see Chapter four, *Our own worst enemy*).

The butterfly rule

When going into the deposition, a physician defendant frequently knows that he upheld the highest standard of care. A mistake medical personnel are inclined to make violates what I call *The Butterfly Rule*. I named this after one of my favorite actresses, Butterfly McQueen. We will recall her famous line in the Hollywood epic, *Gone With The Wind*, where after her character, Prissy, has bragged to Scarlett about her midwifery experience, she breaks down and confesses she knows nothing about birthing babies.

Simply stated, the Butterfly Rule reads: *It is unwise for a witness to ever admit to being an expert about anything, even if others perceive him as such.* A physician may be the best cardiologist in the country and have the honors to prove it, but in a court of law the ego and reputation have to be left outside.

The physician will find it easier to defend the common denominator than justify a management that is too esoteric for a judge or jury to understand. The old "for I'm the greatest, so I must be right" attitude does not hold up well in deposition. That kind of overconfidence makes the witness susceptible to traps. The plaintiff's counsel will find a witness with less experience to testify that our cardiologist is fallible, and the half-life of the defense will be shorter than Adenosine's.

The opposite is also true. It may support our need for humility, but I hate to see a physician claim that he is *not* an expert. Expert status is not a condition we can decide for ourselves; it is bestowed upon us by others. A physician may be considered an expert based on experience, number of publications, reputation, or simply because his mannerisms and flow of speech suggest worldly knowledge. A doctor who specifically denies expertise in a field, especially one in question in a lawsuit, may lose credibility with the judge or jury. The witness should simply relate education, training, and experience, and let the court decide whether or not these meet the qualifications for an expert.

It has been my opinion for years that most health care providers practice a level of care that is above that considered standard. In front of a plaintiff's lawyer, however, a witness may feel insecure and concerned that he has been delivering substandard care. The lawyer will play on these insecurities and push the witness into defining a standard much higher than he can hope to attain. An example from such a deposition follows:

LAWYER: What was Rosa's temperature at 8:00 a.m.?

WITNESS: Unfortunately, I did not record it.

> LAWYER: What was her temperature at 8:15?
>
> WITNESS: Unfortunately, I did not record any temperatures.

It would be easy for this plaintiff's lawyer to convince the jury that this health-care professional deviated from the standard of care because he admits that the temperature should have been taken by qualifying his responses with *unfortunately*. The poor witness felt that he was negligent and was brow-beating himself for not thinking to take the temperature when, in fact, it may not have been standard to take a temperature at all under the existing circumstances. To answer more frankly and to the point, i.e., "I did not take the temperature," or simply, "I don't know what the temperature was," puts the burden of proof back on the plaintiff's lawyer to find someone who will testify that not taking the temperature at that point was deviating from the standard of care.

The same holds true for testimony surrounding the *celebrities* in the medical field. Attorneys will encourage the witness to recognize a written reference or the author as an *authority* to build a case for the defendant's deviant action. This is similar to a tactic lawyers use to discredit the testimony of expert witnesses in personal injury complaints.

If the witness admits to the validity of the scientific method, the lawyer can use this to his advantage in the courtroom. It does not take a degree from MIT to convince a jury that the witness's conclusion cannot possibly be derived using the scientific method.

If a witness in a malpractice deposition is driven to accept any outside source as gospel, it will not be long before the plaintiff's counsel will turn that source against the defendants. Any text or person a health care provider considers useful as a resource can be easily elevated to the level of *authority*. In the following example, I was being questioned in my role as an outside consultant during a hearing:

> LAWYER: Dr. Uribe, are you familiar with the Atlas of Surgery?
>
> WITNESS: Which one specifically?
>
> LAWYER: The one by Zollinger.
>
> WITNESS: Yes.
>
> LAWYER: Do you consider Dr. Zollinger an authority when it comes to surgical procedures?
>
> WITNESS: I don't know, I never met him.
>
> LAWYER: This atlas is considered by many to be authoritative, isn't that true?

WITNESS: There are many texts that offer information.

LAWYER: Then, do you believe Dr. Halsted was an expert in the field of surgery?

WITNESS: I never met him, either. He died long before I was born.

LAWYER: Are you familiar with his statement... (reads lengthy quote from text)? Do you agree or disagree with this statement?

WITNESS: I disagree.

LAWYER: Why is that?

WITNESS: What was true at the turn of the last century is not necessarily true today.

The lawyer wanted me to acknowledge both the atlas and one of our major pioneers in surgery as current authorities and I refused to do so. If all patients were treated according to a book, we would not need lengthy residency training programs.

Occasionally, the lawyer may want the witness to define his own authorities as demonstrated in the following:

LAWYER: Do you know of any text, authority, or policy on when you would use a nasal cannula, non-rebreather mask or a bag valve mask?

WITNESS: That would be objective, on an individual basis.

LAWYER: So what you're telling me is you don't know of any written authority or policy on that?

WITNESS: I think there are probably text considerations, but policies per se, I would not.

LAWYER: Do you know what the texts say on when you should use nasal cannula vs. non-rebreather mask vs. bag valve mask?

WITNESS: I can't be specific without the text in front of me.

The lawyer clearly wanted to pin down the witness to a specific source of information he would consider authoritative. The job would be clearly defined for the attorney — find where the witness's action differed from that mentioned in the authority. Later in the deposition the lawyer tried again:

> LAWYER: Do you know of any authority that says when to use a bag valve mask vs. using a non-rebreather mask or a nasal cannula and at what point, when someone is having respiratory difficulties?

> WITNESS: I think it's an objective decision based on the other accompanying factors.

The witness continued to resist mentioning a specific reference since doing so would automatically deem it an authority. He also offers his awareness that each patient has to be evaluated as an individual, something that is always impressive to a jury.

If a witness wants to accept a text or an author as authoritative, it behooves him to read that text and everything else written by the author to protect himself from the embarrassment of discovering his action deviated from the standards as recommended by that authority. Explaining how your management is supported in the literature is easier than trying to justify any discrepancies in your approach from those found in gilded treatises.

The code of the sinking ship

Physicians tend to view the management of a patient *in toto*, so to speak. This is because we rely on our colleagues for their expertise in dealing with difficult problems. When a lawsuit is filed and the defendants are served, there is a tendency to ask, "Where did *we* go wrong?" and "How could they do this to *us*?" This type of camaraderie is unknown in the legal profession.

Each physician involved will have a lawyer for his defense. There will be no lawyer defending the medical profession per se, and each one of the lawyers assigned will have only one task: to prove to the fact-finders that his client is free of any blame for the harm that came to the plaintiff. The lawyer does not really care about the other defendants except insofar as the weight of their liability measures up to his client's.

Hence, *The Code of the Sinking Ship*: It's every man for himself. Physicians will be told not to discuss the case in question with anyone, especially others named in the lawsuit. Many friendships have probably been severed because one lawyer was adamant about placing the blame on another defendant to shift the liability away from his client.

One young physician came whimpering to me because he had been named a *non-party at fault* in a malpractice case. He was advised of this by the attorney who was hired to sit with him during his deposition. This particular doctor was never served with a complaint but was upset, never-theless, because one of the defendant doctors, during the deposition, mentioned that acts by this physician could have contributed to the patient's problem. Our young doctor was angry that another colleague had turned against him.

Upon review of the deposition, the witness never made any such statement. The accusations of the young doctor's possible involvement came directly from questions asked by the lawyers representing the other physicians named in the suit as well as the plaintiff. The defendant felt guilty about this as it was never his intention to implicate anyone.

A nurse told me of a deposition she had given in front of a whole panel of lawyers. The plaintiff was suing the hospital and 26 doctors. Each doctor had his lawyer hanging on her every word in hopes of getting enough information to clear his respective client. No one would make a motion picture about this. It is entirely too frightening.

Summary

During a deposition, it is not our place to define the standard of care. A court of law will do that for us. What we can do is testify truthfully and accurately so as to keep the standard to which we will be held *reasonable* and *ordinary*.

References

Douthwaite, G., *Jury Instructions on Medical Issues*, The Allen Smith Company, 1980.
Spiegel, A. D. and Kavaler, F., American's first medical malpractice crisis, 1835-1865, *Journal of Community Health*, 22, 283, 1997.

chapter four

Our own worst enemy

"The doctor is in court on Tuesdays and Wednesdays."

overheard at a doctor's office

Malpractice lawsuits are not won or lost at deposition. The attorneys approach this part of the lawsuit as another process leading toward the trial. The main objective is to get the defendant in a courtroom so that the members of the jury will see why he or she deserves to be burned at the stake. Since the plaintiff's hired gun is always willing to deal with the issue in a more civilized manner, a settlement in the form of a huge sum of money will be quite satisfactory. If that settlement is equal to the full value of the defendant's deep pocket, so much the better.

On occasion, the plaintiff's case falls under the old *res ipsa loquitur* — the thing speaks for itself. The inadvertent removal of the wrong leg or the retained hemostat in the patient's abdomen falls under this category. However, when the complaint is not so clear-cut, the plaintiff must acquire the assistance of another physician who will present the evidence to the jury in such a way that there can be no doubt of the defendant's negligence or incompetence. This physician can quickly become the fuel injector behind the plaintiff's motivation.

The expert witness

Believe it or not, the most important quality a lawyer looks for in an expert has little to do with his qualifications: It is how well he will come across to the jury. Just as a patient will frequently choose a physician by his personality, good looks, or tendency to spend a little extra time explaining things, the jury may bond with the charismatic doctor on the witness stand and believe everything he says despite a lack of actual experience with the issue or even questionable credentials.

A physician who pads his credentials, gives false testimony, or alters the known standards to suit the side writing the check can ruin an innocent defendant's reputation. Insurance carriers may be quick to settle or the defendant may push for an unjustified settlement out of fear (see Chapter five, *Weighing the alternatives*).

The worst scenario, of course, is a jury verdict against an innocent physician, especially if large sums of money are awarded. Any action taken against the physician necessitates a report to the National Practitioner Data Bank. It remains branded on the doctor like an "A" on Hester, and he will be reminded of it every time an application for appointment or licensure is made.

A seasoned malpractice lawyer will carefully screen his experts before having the medical record reviewed and/or other depositions studied. Most physicians willing to testify for plaintiffs in malpractice cases charge between $200 and $300 an hour for a case review and $300 to $500 per hour for deposition testimony, so the lawyers working on a contingency basis will check into their track records first.

A doctor whose testimony was instrumental in obtaining a sizable jury verdict for a plaintiff is sure to be used again for a similar case. The prepared lawyer will be willing to shell out $1500 to $5000 per day to get this person on the witness stand to support his plaintiff's case.

An expert witness needs to come across to the jury as honest and sincere. It must appear that his only goal in life at that moment is to remain neutral but, at the same time, right the horrible injustice done to a poor unsuspecting patient. The same is true for the defense expert: That witness, with absolute neutrality, has the task of convincing a jury that the physician has been wrongly accused.

Dr. Jessica Johnston, a pioneer in the specialty of Emergency Medicine, related an experience she had many years ago as an expert witness testifying on behalf of a doctor being sued for complications arising from a dog bite. Johnston was giving testimony supporting the defendant's management when counsel for the plaintiff tried to discredit her testimony by repetitively quoting an article printed two years prior.

Frustrated with his persistence, she turned to the jury and said, "I guess I just don't know. I'm just a country doctor trying to do the best I can." The jury was sympathetic to the demands of a country doctor, and Johnston's honesty was a deciding factor in the jury's decision to bring in a defense verdict.

Juries are apt to trust people who are physically attractive and confident. These characteristics equate with success in our subconscious. It stands to reason that background and credentials should be taken into consideration, but an expert's education and experience can be dealt with quickly and the jury may only need to be assured that he is an M.D. or D.O.

Unfortunately, in most states those initials after a person's name are all that are needed to get an individual on the witness stand. The expert need not be trained in the same field as the defendant nor does he need to be active in the practice of medicine.

An internist with subspecialty training and years of experience was sued for malpractice. The only witness willing to speak out against her was a non-boarded physician whose background was occupational medicine. Fortunately, his demeanor was as weak as his credentials and the jury rendered a verdict in favor of the defendant.

Not long after the trial, the expert witness contacted the defendant's attorney saying he would be available if needed for testimony. The lawyer reminded the witness that he only dealt with medical malpractice defense. The doctor explained that he would testify on either side and on any issue.

I recall overhearing lawyers discussing the wonders of a particular expert used by many in the defense of Workmans' Compensation cases. They were commenting that this physician had a remarkable way of explaining things in the courtroom. No matter what actual injury had been sustained by the plaintiff, this witness was always able to convince the jury it was only a contusion.

My personal experience has been, when asked to review a case as a potential lawsuit, to find it easier to defend a doctor's actions than to immediately condemn them. I guess it's the there-but-for-the-grace-of-God-go-I syndrome. Complications and dissatisfaction arise in all fields of medicine and the concepts of breach of duty and causation should be made harder to prove in a court of law than they currently are.

There is also the subject of minority opinion, that which is not generally accepted by the entire medical community but has a certain degree of validity based on scientific principles. In the late 1980s laparoscopic cholecystectomy would have fallen under this category. It was evolving into what would later become the standard of care.

The concept of *reasonable* and *ordinary* must still apply (see Chapter three, *Standard of care*). Because laparoscopic removal of the gallbladder has become commonplace should not imply the laparoscope is the standard for abdominal procedures of any kind. Yet a physician testifying against another should be allowed to express a minority opinion provided it is based on current scientific evidence and distinguished from that which is considered *reasonable* and *ordinary*.

A colleague of mine, an orthopedic surgeon, once remarked that it is possible to defend just about any clinical management if we are willing to spend the time perusing the literature. With the abundance of medical materials available, we can quote data supporting myriad opinions. Any unusual or rare modalities can, with the right preparation, be presented by an expert to an unknowing jury as *reasonable* and *ordinary*.

The importance of a defendant's active role in educating his or her lawyer should be obvious at this point. It will be the lawyer's task to take any erroneous or fallacious remarks and discredit both the witness and the testimony in the eyes of the jury.

Another characteristic lawyers look for in selecting an expert is how intelligently he answers the questions. That does not mean the answers have to be intelligent; they just have to sound intelligent. The witness should appear self-confident without being arrogant and should respond to the questions spontaneously. He must be able to convince a jury that the situation in question is clear and straightforward with answers that are neither invented nor rehearsed.

A clever lawyer will check out a future expert carefully before engaging his services. The lawyer needs to know ahead of time if his witness has any skeletons to hide in his own malpractice litigation history, and the lawyer should know of any action taken by a hospital or licensure board.

Previous trial experience is desirable but not mandatory. It is important that the defendant's counsel research the testimonial history of the plaintiff's hired gun prior to taking his deposition. A defense lawyer should study any prior testimony given by the plaintiff's expert, especially if the case is similar to the one in question. Not only does the lawyer gain a flavor for the way the expert will answer his questions, but such homework will provide counsel with ammunition useful in impeaching the witness at trial. Contradicting testimony serves no purpose other than to fatten the expert witness's bank account.

An orthopedic surgeon was sued for complications arising after an arthroscopic knee procedure. The patient went for a second opinion, and the latter surgeon re-operated on the knee and was happy to serve as the expert witness against the first surgeon. There was a suspicion that the lawsuit was actually instigated by this expert witness.

At deposition, the expert testified that the damage to the patient's knee was caused by the original injury and *possibly*, not *probably*, the post-operative infection contributed to the problem. At trial, the same expert claimed the damage in the knee was due solely to the post-operative infection. Paraphrasing his testimony at trial:

> LAWYER: You ordered an MRI of the knee, is that correct?
>
> WITNESS: Yes, I did.
>
> LAWYER: Did you review that MRI after it was done?
>
> WITNESS: No, I didn't.
>
> LAWYER: Did you go over the report of that MRI?
>
> WITNESS: No, I didn't.
>
> LAWYER: Why didn't you look at the MRI or review the report?
>
> WITNESS: Because I didn't care about the MRI. Have you ever heard of defensive medicine?

This case had an unfortunate outcome in that the judge, a former plaintiff's lawyer, directed a verdict against the orthopedic surgeon. During the pre-trial phase, the judge remarked that he should grant a summary judgment to the defendant, but he did not want to cheat the plaintiff out of his chance in court (see Chapter five, *Weighing the alternatives*). The jury, when polled later, felt the surgeon was innocent of causing any damage to the patient's knee but wondered if it was too late for the patient to sue the expert witness.

Even though a witness may have an exhaustive curriculum vitae and may have written or edited publications in a particular field, a jury will be bored listening to all his wonderful accomplishments. Still, such glowing credentials could serve as leverage to either side during pre-trial settlement conferences. A defendant or his insurance company may feel weak in the knees at the thought of a department head from an ivy-league medical school or training center testifying against him, even though he knows the standard of care was upheld.

A decision to settle could be based solely on the credentials of the opposing expert without even knowing how the witness will perform. A few years ago a physician was initially pleased that a renowned pioneer in the field was willing to testify on his behalf in a malpractice case. The defendant was confident that not only did he comply with the standard of care, but that this witness had more expertise in the area than anyone else and a jury would easily agree.

During the trial the plaintiff's lawyer seated a cocky physician who admitted he lacked the skills necessary to practice in the defendant's environment. The defense had the true expert in the field, but his demeanor was wimpy compared to the witness power on the plaintiff's side. The jury found for the plaintiff.

Testimony from a physician with specialized training in one field against a physician in another specialty is acceptable in Arizona as it is in most states. I could not fathom the depths to which plaintiff's lawyers will dig for witnesses until I was the target of dubious testimony.

Years ago, I was deposed as a witness in a malpractice suit involving two of my fellow physicians and the hospital. When the plaintiff's lawyer wanted to depose me a second time because of my background in credentialing, he had to amend the complaint naming me as a defendant. As the surgical assistant in the case, I was sure the lawyer's request would be denied, but a superior court judge allowed my name to be added to the list without asking for any reason. A year after my deposition I was served with the complaint.

As the new guy in the club, so to speak, I had the right to a change of judges and my request was granted. The new judge did not understand why the lawyer was allowed to add my name to the list, but there was nothing he could do short of denying the plaintiff's lawyer the opportunity to depose me a second time. This left the lawyer with a big problem: To continue the suit against me, he had to find a physician to testify that I deviated from the standard of care.

At the eleventh hour the lawyer for the plaintiff announced his expert, a pediatric anesthesiologist from another state. Curiosity led my husband and me to the site of this expert witness' deposition by my defense counsel.

We drove 300 miles to the place of the deposition. Many times the expert witness will be hours away by air. The defense counsel will usually accommodate the witness and travel to his home territory, but this can put an obvious hardship on the defendant. Still, I believe sitting across the expert during the testimony provides a world of information.

The defendant can see how the witness's appearance along with mannerisms, flow of speech, etc. may come across to a jury. This can be far more valuable than just hearing the defense counsel's opinion of the proceedings or reading the cold written words.

I made one mistake when I attended the expert's deposition. Sitting in a corner away from my lawyer and the witness, I was out of the line of questioning. If faced with this situation in the future, I would park myself right next to my lawyer (unless he objects for some reason) and keep my eyes glued to the witness.

The following exchange took place early in the deposition.

> LAWYER: Do you have any specialized training in surgery or as a surgeon?
>
> WITNESS: No, I don't.
>
> LAWYER: Have you, in fact, ever practiced medicine as a surgeon?
>
> WITNESS: No, I haven't.
>
> LAWYER: Do you have an awareness of the standard of care applicable to surgeons in Anytown?
>
> WITNESS: Yes, I do.
>
> LAWYER: How did you come to have that awareness?
>
> WITNESS: Well, I work with surgeons practically every day, certainly every day that I'm in the operating room and many days that I'm in the Pediatric Intensive Care Unit, so I have a broad and deep exposure to surgical practice.

After hearing this, I decided I could make a fortune testifying against radiologists. I park my car outside radiology at the hospital every morning and walk through the department to get to the operating room. I watch the doctors running those big screens up and down, studying the black and white x-rays, sometimes threading catheters in and out of people. I can honestly testify, "I work with radiologists practically every day, so I have a broad and deep exposure to radiologic practice."

The lawyers hired to defend me had no difficulty recruiting, from other states as well as Arizona, several general surgeons eager to testify on my behalf. None of the surgeons polled criticized my role in the management of the patient. They finally selected a distinguished surgeon with years of experience in quality care issues, but he needed a bit of work. My witness had the unacceptable habit of referring to the plaintiff's expert as "a whore".

Under most circumstances, the plaintiff will be allowed only one expert who testifies that the defendant deviated from the standard of care. A sly malpractice attorney can use the deposition of other physicians, including the defendants, to aid in establishing care standards and in seeking information to reinforce the expert's opinions. The lawyer can also save himself research time if he collects necessary data during a deposition (see Chapter nine, *The inquisition*).

Physicians and other medical personnel can be deposed because of their positions peripheral to the actual malpractice complaint. An example is the plaintiff's lawyer who wants to question the chairman of a medical staff department or credentials committee. The lawyer will usually limit his questions to the physician's involvement in the medical staff affairs related to the doctor or hospital defendants. However, while he has the witness in front of him under oath, the lawyer may attempt to syphon information unrelated to the doctor's actual participation in the case.

In the following example, the doctor being deposed was chairman of a department when the physician defendant was given privileges at the hospital.

> LAWYER: A general question. What's the recommended dosage of Epinephrine for Lisa?
>
> WITNESS: You need an expert if you want to ask these kinds of questions. I'm not an expert witness for you.
>
> LAWYER: Well, whether you be an expert or not, what is the recommended dosage for Lisa?
>
> WITNESS: I'm not going to answer it. I'm not your expert.
>
> LAWYER: Do you know?
>
> WITNESS: Yeah.
>
> LAWYER: What is it?
>
> WITNESS: I'm not going to answer that.

> LAWYER: What is the MAC for Halothane?
>
> WITNESS: I'm not going to answer that either. If you want an expert's testimony, get out your wallet and buy one. I'm not going to be your expert for you.

Teaching can be such a rewarding profession. I was so proud of my pupil when he shared this with me. This doctor knew his contribution to the case was within a limited area, and he decided ahead of time that he was not going to assist the plaintiff's lawyer with his research. He also recognized something was missing; the plaintiff's counsel made no mention of monetary compensation for his expert opinion.

The immunity dilemma

It stands to reason that any expert witness should be held to the same standards in testifying as he is in practicing medicine. When it comes to determining whether or not the physician's testimony under oath is in keeping with standards widely accepted in our profession, the real judge and jury reside in peer review. A witness giving false or misleading testimony should be subjected to the same scrutiny that exists in daily practice.

In this example we see testimony from a plaintiff's expert witness that is clearly contrary to known medical standards.

> LAWYER: What is bigeminy?
>
> WITNESS: It is PVCs, having two of them in a row, and then a normal complex and then two coming again.

Further along in the same deposition, the lawyer for the defendant asks questions regarding the correct management of a cardiac arrest with asystole on the monitor:

> WITNESS: Even the Atropine really should have been readily available and given first.
>
> LAWYER: I understand.
>
> WITNESS: And that should have been, you know, given. And within 15, 20, 30 seconds. If you didn't see a response in a full arrest situation, the patient should have been given the Epinephrine right there.

As an Affiliate Faculty of the Arizona Heart Association, I have developed Advanced Cardiac Life Support courses in my area and have actively participated in teaching these courses throughout this state and Nevada. I can say with some conviction that the above expert's definition of "bigeminy" is incorrect. Also, it is widely accepted that Epinephrine is the first drug to be given in an arrest situation, not Atropine.

The judge and jury are the fact-finders. It is their job to tell the world what the facts are based upon the evidence they receive. The above testimony could be presented in court and a jury could pass judgment based upon these erroneous statements. In a court of law, the above would be presented as *evidence* and the jury would establish the *facts*.

We physicians have no control over the discipline of those peers who misinterpret or create new standards. Expert witnesses have always been immune from punitive action. Any attempt to report or merely inform a state medical board of such deviant testimony has been met with failure.

David T. Thornton, Supervising Investigator II with the Discipline Coordination Unit of the Medical Board of California, writes, "The Board has no specific jurisdiction in regard to expert witnesses. The testimony of an expert witness stands on the basis of the information provided. It is the responsibility of the attorney who represents the opposing side to impeach the expert witness's testimony if it is not accurate and to point out significant discrepancies."

Therefore, it becomes a battle of wits between counsel on opposing sides. Whether the defendant is innocent or liable is not the issue; the jury will believe whichever side is more convincing. And the licensing body, like Lady Justice herself, wears a blindfold.

Hope for the future

The reason for freedom in expert witness selection stems from the perceived difficulty of obtaining physicians to testify against each other. By refusing to speak out in situations of questionable actions on the part of our colleagues, it seems we have opened a Pandora's box of renegade doctors whose main pastime is making runs to the bank.

It would be nice to think if we banded together and took hold of the situation, testimonial abuse would disappear. The process is not quite that easy. For years organizations such as the American College of Obstetricians and Gynecologists, the American Association of Neurological Surgeons, the American Academy of Orthopaedic Surgeons, and the American College of Pediatrics had guidelines related to expert testimony. Until recently there has been no actual recourse against physicians who sway juries away from recognized standards of care.

Concerned physicians in Florida organized an Expert Witness Committee (EWC) to investigate complaints related to such testimony. According to Drs. Luria and Agliano, "It is the premise of the Hillsborough County Medical Association that it alone is the ultimate bastion in determining the true standard of care in Hillsborough County, Florida, whether in medical practice or expert testimony. We will not allow these standards to be bastardized in the office, hospital or courtroom."

This EWC appoints a panel of physicians to review the expert's testimony, whether given at trial or deposition, and complaints deemed valid are forwarded to the state licensing board. It is, of course, mandatory that the state pass legislation giving its board the power to act on these complaints.

Luria and Agliano explain that experts testifying on behalf of either the plaintiff or defendant are given equal and impartial consideration. It is not the intent of the EWC to discourage doctors from testifying when appropriate since "the medical profession is expected to police itself for all varieties of misconduct that bring the profession into disrepute." In fact, if the committee feels that the expert witness upheld the standard of care in his/her testimony and the complaining physician's management fell below that standard, the complainant is referred to the state medical board for review.

In 1998 the American Medical Association adopted recommendations aimed at expert witness testimony. The AMA is now encouraging each state medical society to work with its state licensing board toward developing effective disciplinary measures for physicians who provide fraudulent testimony. This should also include programs designed to discipline physicians for unprofessional conduct relative to their testimony.

Twenty-eight of our states currently have licensing boards that define the practice of medicine broadly enough to include expert witness testimony. Our state medical associations in conjunction with licensing boards should work with the legislatures in rewording the statutes to allow action against testimonial abuse.

The AMA also suggests each state licensing board grant a temporary license (perhaps at no cost) to any out-of-state expert witness on a per case basis. This would allow the board to address problems with out-of-state witness' testimony and subject those witnesses to the state's peer review process.

An EWC should be formed in each state to develop a program using the one in Florida as a model. The AMA has made a commitment to support each state medical association in its quest to form an Expert Witness Committee program.

The ten commandments of testimony

We have a responsibility to protect the public from disease and from ourselves. The first part we assume with ease, the second is much more sensitive. Anyone seduced into the prospect of testifying against another physician should be sure his testimony is honest and truthful and in the best interest of the patient.

I, therefore, offer "The Ten Commandments of Testimony". I have followed these guidelines in my own practice and you may find them helpful in yours.

1. Thou shalt have like education and training as the physician thou art planning to testify against.
2. Thou shalt be in the active practice of medicine and shalt have experience with the same medical issue in question.
3. Thou shalt not hold the defendant physician to a standard other than that which is considered reasonable and ordinary.
4. Thou shalt deliver testimony that is honest, truthful, and with a neutral attitude based upon undisputed clinical and/or scientific evidence.
5. Thy testimony at trial shall deviateth not from that given in deposition.
6. Thou shalt not practice addressing the jury by selling shoes to snakes.
7. Thy testimony shall be in the best interest of the patient.
8. Thou shalt not receive more than 20% of thy yearly income from testimony.
9. Thou shalt not receive reimbursement for time spent or testimony based upon the eventual outcome of the case.
10. Thou shalt not talk during breaks in the trial about thy planned trip to Switzerland.

Summary

Expert witnesses are not selected by plaintiff's lawyers solely on the basis of their knowledge or credentials. Human factors play a major role in expert witness selection. Because of the impropriety of some witnesses when testifying during medical malpractice depositions and trial, a move is currently underway to hold those witnesses accountable to licensing boards since their testimony should constitute the practice of medicine and should be in accordance with recognized standards.

References

Brallier, J. M., *Lawyers and Other Reptiles*, Contemporary Books, 1992.
Cohen, L. J., Better examination of medical experts, Continuing Legal Education Options, 1998.
Luria, L. W. and Agliano, D. S., Abusive expert testimony: Toward peer review, Civil Justice Memo, The Manhattan Institute, April, 1997.
Thornton, D. T., personal communication, 1997.
Wilder, J., Choosing the right expert witness, *Family Advocate*, 12, 44, 1990.

chapter five

Weighing the alternatives

"If they ever give you a brief, attack the medical evidence. Remember, the jury's full of rheumatism and arthritis and shocking gastric troubles. They love to see a medical man put through it."

John Mortimer,
advising law students

The Data Bank. The dreaded National Practitioner Data Bank. It was created through Title IV of Public Law 99-660, the Health Care Quality Improvement Act of 1986. The original intent of the Data Bank was to improve the quality of health care by identifying problem practitioners and preventing incompetent physicians and other medical professionals from moving state to state leaving their dirty laundry behind.

Acting as a clearing house of information since 1990, the NPDB holds data pertaining to licenses, clinical privileges, and professional society memberships. It is mandatory to report any disciplinary action by state boards such as censures, suspensions, or revocations of licenses; any restriction of clinical privileges by a hospital or Health Maintenance Organization; any action taken by a professional society through a formal peer review process; any voluntary relinquishing of privileges by a practitioner during an investigation; and any malpractice payments made on behalf of a practitioner as the result of settlement or judgment.

Along with state licensing boards, hospitals, and HMOs, other health care entities may query the Data Bank as they deem necessary. If the entity is in the business of providing health care and engages in peer review activity, it meets the criteria necessary to access the Data Bank.

Confidentiality of the information in the Data Bank is protected by law. The Office of Inspector General has the authority to impose civil monetary penalties, up to $10,000 for each party responsible, for violation of the confidentiality provisions of Title IV. Anyone who is listed in the Data Bank may obtain his own information and is permitted to share it with whomever he chooses.

For any health care provider who has been given a place in the Data Bank after a settlement or jury verdict from an unwarranted complaint, the only redeeming factor is the blank space at the bottom of the reported information in which the practitioner can explain his side of the story. This entry is also confidential and released only to hospitals, state licensing boards, and the other health care entities which have a right to see it.

The information is not available to the public or any attorney on a scavenger hunt. Still, the physician who is listed in the Data Bank will be asked to report this fact every time he or she applies for privileges or licensure, and hospitals are obligated by law to query the Data Bank at the time of a health care provider's application or renewal of privileges.

Since the original purpose of the NPDB was to identify problem practitioners, it is natural to assume that inclusion in this selective list equates with incompetence. This conclusion has not only been shown to be erroneous, but studies have been hard pressed to demonstrate a relation between the amount of settlement or judgment and deviation from care standards.

A place in the Data Bank does not, in itself, equate with bad medical practice. In fact, when I was singing the blues over my own entry, a colleague remarked, "You're in good company." Regardless of the circumstances, being in the *Hall of Infamy* is a blow to the ego.

The Dirty Harry principle

It is my opinion that medical malpractice litigation rarely has anything to do with the bad practice of medicine. *Medical dissatisfaction* would be a more appropriate term. The complainant is unhappy with an outcome and wants compensation in the form of money. Plaintiff counsel rarely understand why physicians and nurses take malpractice lawsuits so seriously since we have liability insurance. I am sure that most attorneys would rather deal directly with the insurance carrier, but we doctors react as if we were wrongly accused of assault, battery, or even homicide.

The fact is that 70-80% of all medical malpractice cases taken to court result in verdicts favoring the defendants and most of the ones lost bring in judgments less than those offered at pre-trial settlements. Even so, most physicians and nurses, when hit with a lawsuit, will accuse the plaintiff of *blackmail*. That's such an ugly word.

I like to think of malpractice litigation more as a form of *extortion*. It's as if the lawyer puts a gun to the doctor's head and says, "You have a million dollars sitting in your liability carrier's bank, and I want it now!" This is when the doctor applies the Dirty Harry Principle; he must ask himself, "How lucky do I feel?"

He can tell his carrier to give the thief the money, or he can grab the gun and take his chances on winning the fight that is guaranteed to ensue.

Depending on the conditions of the policy, the doctor may or may not have a say in the matter.

Many carriers will take a case to trial if the doctor insists, with the understanding that any judgment over the policy limits will have to be borne by the insured. This decision should not be made without careful consideration of all possible outcomes. The significance of this is of prime importance in lawsuits involving infants, children, and any events that reek of sensationalism. Again, the Dirty Harry Principle applies.

Blood money

My girlfriend was called to testify in a criminal trial. Her friend was accused of first-degree murder. A teenager was missing and his church offered a sizable reward for any information concerning his whereabouts. Even though a body was never found, a woman came forth testifying that she heard the accused admit to killing the boy.

My friend is a stunning lady and she sat on the witness stand dressed to the nines: vintage dress, hat, gloves, the whole enchilada. As one observer put it, she looked like Jackie O. Her voice was soft with a musical, almost childlike quality, and her nervousness was partly concealed by the prosecutor's promise he would go easy on her.

When the interrogator began touting the pristine qualities of the woman who had blown the whistle, the witness — knowing the woman, the motive behind her accusation, and the sensationalism surrounding this trial — blurted out, "She's a slut! She wears shorts so short you can see her pubic hair!" The jury was shocked to hear such words coming from this elegant lady, but my friend's honest candor was sufficient to quickly bring in a not-guilty verdict.

The man accused of this crime was a fashion designer, small in stature to begin with, and frail from his underlying AIDS. He would not have been able to overpower the larger, stronger teenager who was missing, much less dispose of the body.

The designer died not long afterward, but I'm sure the year he spent in jail awaiting trial added stress to his already damaged immune system. His creations still grace my closet as well as my body on festive occasions. They are a reminder, not of this grueling ordeal, but of his talent and our mutual friend who was eager to do anything to prove his innocence.

If we are unable to draw any similarity between the accused above and a doctor or nurse sitting at the defendant's table in a malpractice trial, it only reflects our inexperience. As Dr. Abraham Kuruvilla put it, "During my trial I felt like something was coming over me, pulling me under water." This physician watched as his professional life was tried, convicted, and executed in a court of law.

His *prosecutors* did not care what physical or emotional strains were placed on him and his family. They only wanted the money. They sought to prove liability, but to the defendant it was a matter of guilt or innocence.

Kuruvilla was a successful, renowned neonatologist in Phoenix. In 1985, he accepted a 37-week newborn male in transfer. The patient had transient tachypnea and persistent pulmonary hypertension of the newborn. He gave the infant a combination of AB plasma with 0 negative red cells to aid in perfusion and diuresis, and the baby recovered over the next few days.

Approximately a year and a half later, Kuruvilla was informed by the Blood Bank through their Look Back Program of the probability of HIV contamination in the blood given the baby. In 1985, there was no way of testing the donated blood for HIV. He informed the baby's parents as well as the pediatrician caring for him, by phone and in writing. He discovered the parents had already been made aware.

The lawsuit was filed by the parents as representatives of the child who was very ill at the time. When the subject of settlement arose, the insurance company offered $50,000 and the plaintiffs asked for $500,000. The insurer upped the offer to $150,000 and the plaintiffs upped their demand to 1 million. The insurance carrier, at that point, was so convinced of Kuruvilla's innocence of any wrongdoing, that a decision was made to litigate to completion.

The judge originally agreed to conditions of the bifurcated trial: one for deciding liability and one for deciding damages. The first part of the trial would be completed without the jury seeing the child. Only if Kuruvilla was found liable for malpractice would the jury be exposed to the child to aid in assessing damages. Much to Kuruvilla's surprise, the judge changed his mind and allowed the child in the courtroom once during the first phase of the trial.

In 1990, Kuruvilla was sitting in the defendant's chair listening as the expert witness for the parents testified that a consent for the transfusion should have been obtained even though in 1985 it was not the standard of care to do so. In fact, Kuruvilla's lawyer was able to produce affidavits from teaching institutions around the country showing 66% of them were not obtaining consents as late as 1989.

The plaintiffs also denied ever being contacted by Kuruvilla. That complaint was dropped, but only after a subpoena produced the copy of the letter sent to the pediatrician.

Kuruvilla's expert witness was a learned physician who had exhaustive research credits to his name. It was not difficult for him to testify about the appropriateness of the blood and plasma combination in this critically ill newborn, but he was a soft-spoken man who was in stark contrast to the cocky plaintiff's expert.

One of the jurors was a woman obviously in a family condition herself. Hearing the details of the plaintiff's birth and post-partum complications undoubtedly had a negative impact on this pregnant juror. Kuruvilla carefully watched the reactions of the other jury members to the testimony as well as the presence in their midst of this woman with an unborn child.

The plaintiff's counsel spent hours on both his opening and closing statements. The defense counsel made a 90-minute opening statement so convincing it defused the dramatic ambience for a news reporter covering the trial. It seemed clear early in the proceedings that the actual validity of the complaint should be questioned.

Even though the defense attorney's closing statement lasted for only minutes, the plaintiff's lawyer objected to most of the remarks. The jury deliberated several hours before handing down an unfavorable verdict for Kuruvilla.

The second phase of the trial lasted for more than a week. During this time numbers were the stars of the show. One expert testified the patient had a life expectancy of 40 years. An actuarial for the plaintiff estimated $600,000 per year would be needed to care for the patient, and the expert for the defense spoke of $48,000 a year until the last year of life which would cost $96,000.

The jury rendered a judgment of $26.7 million for the patient and $1 million for each parent, bringing the total liability for Kuruvilla to $28.7 million. The hospital was found liable for another $200,000 and the Blood Bank $1.7 million.

Then the question of process arose. There were technical points about the way the trial was conducted that could warrant investigation by a higher court. The plaintiffs, knowing such an appeal would be forthcoming, decided to settle for a much lesser amount: $6 million, if the defense would decline the option to appeal.

"At that point, I had no financial loss if I chose to settle. I just wanted to get on with it, but my life was over as a neonatologist." Kuruvilla packed up his family and left for a much-deserved vacation in a small village in his native India. (The amount of the judgment was more than that state's entire budget.)

Kuruvilla was out of the country when the physicians and their families marched on the Capitol Building in Phoenix, yet he was appreciative of the support he had from his colleagues during and after the trial. Even the news media changed their tune as proceedings went along.

In retrospect, the expert witness for the plaintiff was never asked to define the standard of care. "What you see as doing nothing wrong, an expert can show an ignorant jury as otherwise." Kuruvilla explained, "It took me awhile to learn the difference between facts and evidence."

After the smoke settled, Kuruvilla completed a family practice residency and holds his boards in that field. "I only see well babies now," he explains. He lost his dream of giving care to helpless, critical infants; the rest of society lost a gifted intensivist.

Making the fat lady sing

The word *settle* has several meanings, many of which pertain to malpractice litigation: bring to rest; fix or resolve conclusively; take up an ordered or stable life; sink to the bottom. The last definition is meaningful to any doctor or nurse who has been singled out by a patient and accused of negligence with or without malicious intent.

The fact is most civil lawsuits come to settlement. Most civil lawsuits, however, do not accuse doctors or nurses of wrongdoing, nor do they risk a report to the National Practitioner Data Bank. The only advantage, if there is one, to settling a malpractice case is closure. It (that is, the case itself) will be over, finished, kaput. The pain many physicians feel after settlement never really dies, but that which does not kill us is supposed to make us strong.

There is a built-in benefit for plaintiff lawyers to reach a sizable settlement. If the case goes to trial and the plaintiff is lucky enough to walk away with an enormous award in the form of periodic payments, the lawyer may be stuck with his share being doled out a little at a time as well. A pre-trial settlement will give the lawyer his share in one lump sum.

It is not uncommon for a physician, months or years after a case has been settled by his carrier, to look back with regret at not fighting the complaint to the limits of the law, if he had the choice to do so at the time. Regrettably, the Dirty Harry Principle no longer applies after the fact. ·

This regret is not so much felt with a clearer head as it is contemplated at a time when the option is not an issue. The doctor's assets are not at risk at this point and the emotionally charged atmosphere surrounding a complaint in progress is absent. We tend to focus on the ideal justice system and it simply does not exist. Hindsight, when it comes to malpractice cases, is not always 20/20.

The late lawyer-ethicist Charles P. Curtis once wrote that the administration of justice is no more designed to elicit the truth than the scientific approach is designed to extract justice from the atom. The purpose of taking a case to court is to put an end to it once and for all and, at the same time, have the dispute decided in a fair and equitable manner. Well, King Solomon isn't going to be there in the courtroom. The defendant's definition of what's fair and the court's may be at opposite ends of the spectrum.

I recall a case I settled years ago. The primary physicians directly involved with the patient were sued and I, as the assistant surgeon, was added to the complaint at a much later date. The other parties in the case had settled. One of the doctors told me, "I'm willing to take the chance on losing, but I can't do this to my wife."

I had the same insurance carrier as Dr. Kuruvilla and I almost expected an override of my suggestion for settlement as they did in his case. After all, my case did not have the stark sensationalism of Kuruvilla's. I later asked the claims representative handling my case why the company rolled over and wrote the check. He answered, "Dr. Smith said in deposition he thought you were running the show." The carrier had learned a bitter lesson from the Kuruvilla case, and this piece of evidence alone was enough to make them shy away from another possibly sympathetic jury.

Since the plaintiff was unable to find a surgeon in this country who would testify against me (the expert knew nothing about surgery), and even the plaintiff's expert testified that my actions were above and beyond the standard of care, why on earth did I choose to settle and why did the insurer quickly abide by my wish? All the factors were weighed before making the decision.

First, I had aggressive lawyers who had been successful in the courtroom defending doctors on many occasions. Second, any question of my involvement in the case could be explained easily to lay jurors, and there was enough evidence that I felt any jury in its right mind would give me a medal along with my verdict of innocence. Also, at that point in time there had never been a jury verdict against a physician in the county in which I reside. I grew up in this town and I had an enviable reputation.

On the other hand, the plaintiff had a set of raptors, or rather lawyers, who were not used to losing in the courtroom either. And the life I saved was that of a brain-damaged child. Having been deposed by one of these lawyers, I could tell by his questioning that he wanted so badly to connect my mere presence in the patient's room to the outcome.

The judge who allowed the complaint to be amended with my name as a new defendant was quickly taken off the case. The newly assigned judge seemed very sympathetic and did not understand why I was added since it was clear I was only the assistant surgeon. He obviously had a handle on the matter, or so I thought.

The same judge initially granted a summary judgment in my favor. The plaintiff's lawyer begged him to reconsider and the judge wrote, "There is an absolute vacuum of testimony to support (plaintiff's) inference." However, to be on the safe side, he vacated the summary judgment.

I figured Factor X, the unknown variable, into the equation. My sixth sense told me to settle even though it was painful to do so. Adding salt to an open wound was less painful than filling out the response in the Data Bank inquiry; but taking into consideration the event that followed, I'm sure the judge's sympathy for the child outweighed his sense of justice.

Weeks later my goddaughter, a lawyer, had a hearing in front of this judge and reported a conversation she overheard during a break. The judge was shaking his head in dismay and relating his disappointment that my insurance carrier had given so little money to the parents of this poor, brain-damaged child. He did not think it was fair. A court reporter who was present went to my goddaughter and said, "We all know Dr. Uribe did nothing wrong." Had I taken this case to court, it would not have been my actual life on the line: it was only money.

It's easy to say that you know your attorney will eat the plaintiff's expert alive on the stand, but there are many other factors involved that need to be taken into account. For example: Who will wind up on the jury? Are you willing to put the fate of any liability in the hands of total strangers? What if the majority of the jurors hates doctors or just hates the sight of you?

Lawyers and judges have expressed their concerns over the jury's ability to grasp the often complicated aspects surrounding the instructions given after testimony is completed because most jurors have had no formal legal training. I have had concerns over the lay jury's ability to grasp the complicated aspects of medicine, but this is not regarded as a problem for the legal profession. Therefore, are you confident the jurors selected will have the learning skills necessary to comprehend any complex issues, especially if those issues are in question?

The public has come to recognize that jury duty carries a tremendous responsibility, but it also conveys a certain privilege and authority. For some it may be their only shot at 15 minutes of fame, while for others it may fulfill a burning need for control or domination. Will you or your attorney be able to select those individuals whose sole purpose in serving is to see that justice prevails?

How will the jury feel about the plaintiff's lawyer? Will he come across as the silver-tongued serpent he really is, or will he appear to be the patient's savior?

How will your lawyer come across to the jury? Will they resent the way he attempts to impeach the plaintiff's expert?

How will the plaintiff's expert appear in court? Will he be able to deliver testimony that will leave the jury in awe? If the expert is a female, will a mostly male jury succumb to her charm?

How will *your* expert look to the jury? Just how strongly does your expert support your care of the patient?

Who is the judge? What is his or her experience with medical malpractice trials? How do you know the judge didn't have very unpleasant experiences with incompetent doctors as he was growing up? How do you know the judge won't wake up on the wrong side of the bed the day he delivers instructions to the jury?

Is the patient in question dead or alive? Is it a child who will need skilled care for the rest of his life? Can you prove the patient, if deceased, would have had a shortened life span without your involvement?

What is your reputation in the community? How will you look in front of the jury? How will your credentials look? Will you cringe when you see your records blown up for the jury in glorious technicolor and breath-taking cinemascope?

How did you perform in your deposition? Did you make any remarks that you now regret? Did you give any answers that might have a negative impact on a jury or could easily be taken out of context?

How did the other witnesses perform in their depositions? Did anyone's testimony conflict with yours? Did anyone say anything that reflected negatively upon you?

Are you willing to take the time from your practice for a trial that could continue for an unknown period? Will you be able to withstand the stress of the proceedings? Can you maintain your composure while every detail of the case is presented over and over and over again?

How will you feel if you lose? How will you handle a judgment greater than the limits of your policy? Are you willing to risk an appeal and continue the litigation process further?

If you settle, will you regret it later? If you are resistant to settlement, is it because you believe upholding your principles is paramount or you fear an entry in the Data Bank like you fear a felony conviction?

Personally, I do not believe any case with a preponderance of evidence in favor of the health care provider should be settled. Truth and justice, as defined by what is right and what is wrong, should win out. A physician who has delivered care that complies with the standard and has an unforeseen outcome should not be held liable for that outcome. The law, however, is full of uncertainty and no defendant has control of the courts.

Summary

Health care providers who have upheld the standard of care in the management of a patient should never be forced into a settlement with the plaintiff. In reality, however, many factors are involved in the decision to settle or take the case to trial. Among those are the quality and content of all the pretrial depositions, the actual condition of the patient, the character of the jury, and the temperament of the judge. A defendant would be wise to take all of these into consideration prior to rushing into either a major settlement or trial.

References

Brallier, J. M., *Lawyers and Other Reptiles*, Contemporary Books, 1992.

Metter, E.J. and Granville, R.L., The effect of threshold amounts for reporting malpractice payments to the National Practitioner Data Bank: Analysis using the closed claims database of the Office of the Assistant Secretary of Defense (Health Affairs), Military Medicine, 162, 1997.

Rake, B. and Thrasher, B., Medical malpractice myths, truths and solutions, *Arizona Attorney*, 32, 21, 1996.

When Justice is Up to You, Association of Trial Lawyers of America, 1992.

Zobel, H.B. and Rous, S.N., *Doctors and the Law*, W.W. Norton & Company, 1993.

chapter six

Telling the truth

"In order to lie convincingly, a witness must remember every detail of the lie and no one can do that. He knows the truth and it keeps interfering with his story."

Hon. Richard W. Donato

I spent the first four years of life in a small town in southeast Missouri. I recall as a toddler crossing a long living room from the couch, through a wide bedroom and into a huge kitchen where I would always find my grandmother. The trek would take half the day to complete.

After graduation from high school in Arizona, my mother took me back to the town. As we drove down the street I immediately recognized our old home. I ran to the door and knocked. The lady residing in the house was very accommodating and allowed me to enter my old stomping ground. Standing in the living room, I was shocked to discover how it had shrunk over the years! It only took a few steps to go into the kitchen. My recollection of the house differed markedly from reality.

The cherry tree rule

If for some reason I had been plugged into a polygraph machine before visiting the old homestead, I would have described a large, spacious house. I would have been telling the truth, but my description would not have been *accurate*.

I would be violating what I term *The Cherry Tree Rule*: telling the truth, even under oath, is not enough. We must strive for *accuracy* as well. Our perception of things, places, and situations may be clouded and retrieving information from our cerebral data bank can be difficult.

The human data bank

Memory is a nominalization: an action frozen in time, a static phenomenon which cannot be altered or influenced. Therefore, to say we have a good memory or a bad memory is irrelevant because it is the actual process of remembering that is important. (See Chapter eight, *Meeting the inquisitor*, for memory accessing cues.)

Our memory functions on two levels: the conscious and the subconscious. We are more apt to file information in the conscious data bank if that information is of a vital nature. Other perceptions and experiences get buried in the subconscious. Consequently, the conscious file is easier to flip through. The information stored is readily available and our memory is more likely to be accurate. The keeper of the data in our subconscious is sloppy and the information is not always properly catalogued. Experiences from our cumulative past mix and mingle with recently acquired memories, much like a tossed salad.

Let's say that Dr. Jones is finishing evening rounds in the ICU. He is making every effort to be home early on this particular evening to attend a big 50th anniversary party for his in-laws. His wife will accept no excuses for tardiness. Not tonight. She has threatened him with everything from losing his happy home to amputating bodily appendages if he doesn't show for this event.

As Dr. Jones is walking out of the ICU, he is approached by a nurse who asks him to assist Dr. Brown with the patient in Bed 9. Dr. Jones turns and walks toward Bed 9 glancing at his watch. It's now 6:30 p.m. As soon as he arrives at bedside, the patient has a cardiac arrest. A code is called. Other doctors, nurses, and technicians enter the area. After the patient is resuscitated, Dr. Brown thanks Dr. Jones for his help and Dr. Jones walks out of the ICU glancing again at his watch. It reads 6:40 p.m. He has plenty of time to make it home.

A year and a half later, Dr. Jones receives an invitation to give a deposition in a malpractice case against Dr. Brown. He calls Dr. Brown asking what this is all about. The management of the cardiac arrest of the patient in Bed 9 is being questioned. Dr. Jones contacts his liability carrier who provides an attorney to accompany him to the deposition.

In the interrogation Dr. Jones is asked innumerable questions concerning the names and positions of everyone who attended the code. He answers honestly; he can't recall. Then come questions about the pre-arrest condition of the patient. Dr. Jones has to admit he cannot remember any specifics. He has attended many codes over many years and all details pertaining to these incidents are mixed together and he is unable to distinguish this time from any other. They are in the tossed salad of his subconscious file.

Then he is asked, "How long did the code last?" It doesn't take him long to answer, "About 10 minutes." Dr. Jones accurately retrieves that information because it is filed in the conscious data bank along with the anniversary party. He could remember checking his watch because time was vitally important to him that evening.

It is common to store everyday information in the subconscious because it gets to be routine. An example would be a floor plan for an ICU or operating room. We spend many hours a day in these areas, yet if every member of my Department of Surgery were asked to draw a sketch of the layout, I bet we would see 40 different floor plans. They would all be recognizable, but there would be marked differences in detail.

In dealing with a plaintiff's lawyer during a deposition, keep the Cherry Tree Rule in mind. Any testimony can be presented to a judge or jury as fact, so it behooves us to ask ourselves where the answer will be stored since we realize that the subconscious data bank has a faulty retrieval system. This is especially important if the interrogator wants us to comment on someone else's testimony or if he wants our opinion of a drawing made by another witness.

Relying on our memory

During a deposition, we may be able to retrieve information from our conscious system, but our best recollection will be in the form of *documentation*: Whatever is written in the patient's chart is probably what happened at the time. A notation may certainly jog our memory to other details, but the written record can stand up in court as what actually happened.

Asking for further details or elaborating on documentation is a common ploy by plaintiff's lawyers to milk further information from an unsuspecting doctor or nurse. The witness needs to think carefully before offering information that may or may not be entirely accurate. After all, this is not a board exam. There is no need to impress anyone with a vast reservoir of knowledge or feel pressured to make up an answer. Doing so has the potential for harming the innocent.

Any fabricated remark could be used by an aggressive plaintiff counsel to support a claim that the defendant's management was substandard. It was explained to me by a defense lawyer that a deposition is taken under oath and our documentation is not. Therefore, a plaintiff's lawyer might convince a jury that the doctors and/or nurses made notations in the chart in a deliberate attempt to cover up a mishap or a delay. Out-of-court settlements have taken place over deposition testimony that differed from actual documentation.

The defendants in any medical malpractice case have a decided advantage. They were present when the actual events took place, and they are the best source for historical data; however, since our memories are fallible, it is still best to rely on our written documentation. Whatever was written down at the time was probably what actually happened. Occasionally, a case will be dramatic enough to warrant a place in our conscious data bank as demonstrated in the following example.

> LAWYER: Do you remember specifically doing this in Mr. Watt's case, or is this what you normally do?

> WITNESS: In this specific case that is what I recall doing.

LAWYER: How is it that you're able to recall in this specific case exactly what you did?

WITNESS: Only in reflecting on the report and remembering the individual case.

The importance of relying on our documentation and not on our memory is demonstrated in the following deposition. Here the physician is making it clear that documentation is the best source of recall.

LAWYER: Now, on your exam of April 18th when you mentioned the scarring in the ears, do you recall whether you specifically did a physical examination by looking in her ears?

WITNESS: Yes, sir.

LAWYER: Do you have an independent recollection as you sit here of seeing scarring in her ears?

WITNESS: It's six years ago. If I wrote it, it was because I saw it at that time.

The physician does not have to rack her brain and try to recall doing an ear exam on the patient. She wrote the findings down and the record can speak for itself. Her comment, "It's six years ago," tells the lawyer that she is aware of the limitations of accuracy over time.

Another trait of humans is that we are creatures of habit, and the more repetitive our actions, the better programmed our brains and bodies. Practice makes perfect. For example, a person may not remember the details of removing his coat and hanging it in the closet when he first entered his house, but chances are he went through the movements exactly as he has done for years.

We become so accustomed in our daily lives to routines that we subconsciously rely on them. If a patient enters the operating room, there is a better-than-average chance a signed operative consent is on the accompanying chart because that is the way it is always done. During a deposition, questions may arise which could require rummaging through our fallible subconscious data bank save the fact that a routine is involved:

LAWYER: Do you have some way of verifying whether or not this form was in fact given to Mrs. Harrington?

WITNESS: I cannot remember that really. This is normal routine for all my patients.

We are often told that if an action is not written down, a clever attorney will present the premise in court that the action never took place. Be that as it may, if we have a routine we always follow, we have the option of relying on it if a question arises over our action or inaction.

Summary

Truth in testimony is not enough; we must also strive for accuracy in our remarks and recollections. Before answering a question, especially a difficult one, we must ask ourselves where the information is stored, in our conscious or subconscious data bank. If we find it in the subconscious, we must then entertain the possibility that the details may be inaccurate because of the tossed salad effect or simply because of the passage of time. Our documentation as well as the documentation of others is the best evidence to support the correctness of our answers.

Reference

Keeton, R. E., *Trial Tactics & Methods*, Little Brown & Company, 1973.

chapter seven

Preparing for the deposition

> "Be frank and explicit with your lawyer... It is his business to confuse the issue afterwards."
>
> *J. R. Solly*

A written invitation to a deposition creates nervousness and anxiety in members of the medical profession even if no formal complaint of malpractice has as yet been entered. We feel confident in resuscitating the patient in complete cardio-pulmonary arrest, but we cringe at the thought of facing a lawyer's questions. We fear any situation over which we do not have complete control. Teamwork is usually the key to success in medicine, and we have difficulty understanding our duties and responsibilities when confronted with isolation.

Depositions can take several hours or can be divided into multiple sessions. Keeping our guard up for this length of time can put a tremendous strain on us emotionally and physically. Discomfort and nervousness associated with the upcoming deposition can be alleviated if three factors are addressed.

1. Adequate preparation. Discussed in this chapter.
2. Overcoming fear of the unknown. Discussed in more detail in Chapter eight (*Meeting the inquisitor*). The witness will be sitting across from a total stranger, not a patient. The lawyer will probably appear very benign and accommodating, giving the witness a false sense of security. Putting the witness at ease will help establish an atmosphere conducive to full and complete disclosure by the deponent. Remember the snake in the Garden of Eden!
3. Interview with your own lawyer ahead of time. Counsel should take the time to run through possible questions and help the witness develop a feel for what's to come.

The witness may not have been named as a defendant in the case, but this is irrelevant to the preparation. Physicians are notorious for thinking that since they have not been sued, they can relax and go to the deposition with nothing to fear. The plaintiff's lawyer will play on this naívete.

The Boy Scout rule

A young pediatrician contacted me prior to giving a deposition. He had not been named in the lawsuit, but this was his first experience in the legal arena and he wanted to review some of the highlights of my seminar he attended. A week after the deposition, the doctor was served with his own complaint. The date of the filing was actually several weeks before the deposition took place. The plaintiff's lawyer deliberately waited to have this doctor served with the complaint until he had given his testimony. The doctor was aware of such a tactic and was fully prepared. He wrote me later that he was not upset when handed the complaint because he knew he had performed well during the deposition.

Laws vary from state to state and a conference with your lawyer will help to explain the risk of your being added as a defendant at a later date. In Arizona, complaints can be amended and anyone whose name is present anywhere in the records is never completely exempt until a case is closed. This is the basis for *The Boy Scout Rule*: Whether or not you are being sued, prepare for the deposition as if you are!

Unfortunately, many lawyers assume that medical people are educated well enough to know intuitively what is in store for them. A careful description of the environment and other physical aspects of the deposition process will enable the witness to set aside any associated fears and focus on the actual preparation. Too often, a brief meeting with the lawyer will only advise the client to tell the truth, the whole truth, and nothing but the truth. Just answer the questions and do not offer information that has not been requested.

The burden here is on the inquisitor to ask the right questions to elicit information in support of the complainant. The lawyer will try to ask clear, specific questions to commit the witness to a particular position and to obtain admissions. He has only the plaintiff's version of the story, the hospital records, and any office notes, all of which will be used in an attempt to provoke responses to support the accusation.

The importance of documentation

Preparation for a deposition begins at the initial contact with the patient. Few of us approach each medical challenge with the idea that we must prioritize the possibility of a future lawsuit, but the fact remains we must take our documentation practices seriously. We are not just communicating with ourselves and other caregivers anymore. Our written notes help to assure proper reimbursement for services and assist payers in monitoring our utilization of their resources.

Recently, our government has been taking aggressive action against fraud and abuse violations, and our documentation is our best defense if questioned by the federal enforcement agencies. In our media-addictive culture, anything written down also has the potential of being shown on national television.

According to the Risk Management Department of The Mutual Insurance Company of Arizona (MICA), the state's largest insurer, our own documentation frequently presents major defense difficulties. While we would like the jury to see our notes as a carbon copy of what actually took place, they can also be used to show that we are careless, unconcerned, inadequate practitioners, possibly even criminals.

People routinely carry cameras on vacation or to important events. Pictures are taken to document what happens. Years later we may not be able to recall the exact details of an event, but we have a picture to show we were there when the event took place. That is the same purpose our notes serve; they are merely snapshots of what happened, not feature-length motion pictures.

In a court of law, quality of documentation is often equated with quality of care. Reviewing our own records months or even years after the fact can be an enlightening experience. Whatever is documented is what actually happened. What is not written in the medical record is legally presumed not to have occurred. We may not even remember the patient or a particular incident, but our notations and dictations serve as the best reminder of our involvement. Carefully examining our entries and comments will prove invaluable during the deposition.

Next time you finish writing a note on the ward or in your office, stop a second and pretend that it has suddenly been blown up and is being reviewed by a jury of lay people. How does it look? Does it look professional? Have you spelled everything correctly? Is it decipherable?

The first hint of a dissatisfied client can come in the form of a request for records from the soon-to-be plaintiff's lawyer. Lawyer and registered nurse Barbara Hirsch explains, "Whenever possible we have the patient get their own medical records so there is no suspicion that litigation is involved."

It is the policy in my office that the physicians personally review any records that have been requested by a patient or lawyer. A record was once copied and sent to an attorney with an important referral letter missing. It had been misfiled, but the patient had a copy and had given it to her lawyer. I routinely browse through the chart to be sure all entries pertinent to the patient's care are there. This saves embarrassment should I be handed an orphaned part of the record during a deposition or trial.

It is vitally important to refrain from altering the record entries in any way even though we may be tempted to correct a misspelled word or rewrite chicken scratching to make it more legible. Any corrections should be made at the time the note is written with a single line running through the corrected part along with our initials and the date.

A national forensic laboratory is available to lawyers who suspect that a patient's records have been altered. Using fluorescent studies, the actual date of the ink can be determined. For example, a physician added a notation in 1994 (after a lawsuit was filed) to a laboratory report that was dated 1991 in the patient's medical record. By ink-dating analysis, it was confirmed that the notation was written with same ink used in 1994 notes. It is reasonable to believe that a nonexistent or incorrect entry might be easier to defend than a note added years later.

Illegibility is another issue. It has been estimated that 16% of all medical records are impossible to read. Lawyers can insist on legible records and they can ask the court to exclude any records that are undecipherable. Unusually well-organized records wave a red flag in front of a lawyer as well. Physicians are not known for neatness. So we're damned if the entry is too messy and we're damned if it is too tidy.

Human nature causes us to occasionally write comments that have little to do with the patient's actual complaint or clinical condition. It's one thing to "think out loud" in the chart mentioning observations or plausible diagnoses and another to make personal comments, especially those of a disparaging nature. Consider the following entries in office and/or hospital records and imagine how a jury might view the physician author:

- The patient is a 20-year-old female drug addict with no redeeming qualities whatsoever.
- Patient just too fat!
- Patient got pneumo from central line placement; last thing in the world he needed right now.
- Dr. Jones said that patient was Indian and just trying to take advantage of the system. (nurse's note)

Another damaging form of documentation is the written argument. This is usually seen in the hospital record. Physicians and/or support personnel may disagree on a diagnosis or treatment modality, but to voice displeasure in the patient's record is asking for trouble.

An instance comes to mind in which a hospital pharmacist was disagreeing with a physician as to the recipe for a patient's hyperalimentation solution. The note, paraphrased, read:

> I have spoken directly with Dr. Jones and he insists on
> using this formula despite my recommendations and
> he refuses to look at the supporting literature.

The pharmacist may have been thinking he was covering his own tail with the above entry when he may have been putting himself and/or the hospital at risk while, at the same time, becoming a built-in expert witness for the plaintiff against the physician.

Other examples can be found in progress notes from other hospitals.

- Dr. Jones is crazy to send this patient home.
- According to the American Academy of Pediatrics, penicillin should not be used for this problem.
- Patient should be switched to a cephalosporin because it is cheaper.

A mechanism should be in place for hospitals to deal with such conflicts among physicians and hospital personnel. The patient's chart should never be used as a boxing ring.

Other red flags plaintiffs' lawyers look for in reviewing records include

- Incomplete records or incomplete entries. If, for some reason, our attention becomes diverted before we complete our notes, we must remember to go back right away and finish writing them.
- Too many supplements added to the records. Squeezing little notes in the margins or between lines leads the reader to believe you made later entries.
- Unavailability of the original records. Lack of availability of requested records supports a lawyer's argument for a physician's deviation from standard of care. After all, with no hard documentation, it's the patient's word against ours. Patients see a few doctors in their lifetimes, physicians see hundreds of patients. The jury will trust the patient's memory over ours.
- Excessively consistent records. It's only human to have little inconsistencies in thinking and documentation, especially with a complicated problem. The chart should not look as if it were compiled after the fact.
- Blank spaces. This will look as if the physician planned to "pad" the entries with information or was simply careless and forgot to go back and enter important details.
- Duplicate records. Especially if they are contradictory.

The bottom line is we must scribble as if we're writing in a hurry, but it must be legible; we need to document events as they occur, even if there is a little inconsistency in our observations or thought process; all spaces have to be filled in at the time of entry so that our writing habits are immediately identifiable and consistent throughout the record; and no creative record keeping is allowed.

The last item, duplicate records, would be a favorite of mine if I were a lawyer. I would love to see two of anything: two discharge summaries, two operative notes, etc. This is where the efficiency of the hospital's Medical Records Department comes into play.

I sat through 30 minutes of a deposition as a surgical resident answering questions over and over again as to why there were two discharge summaries on the chart. One was done by my intern when the patient left the hospital and the other was dictated by me six months later when Medical Records could find no trace of the first one. As luck would have it, the original summary eventually hit the chart and, needless to say, mine was the shorter of the two. The dictations did not contradict each other, but the lawyer quizzed me on very minute differences in the reports.

Any duplicate entries should be complementary without discrepancies in the data. If two operative reports dictated six months apart are given to a plaintiff's lawyer and there is a discrepancy as to the type of suture used in the operation, the witness needs to be prepared to explain the reason for the different documentation.

Not mentioned in the list is correspondence unrelated to the patient's specific diagnosis or treatment; that is, any material received by the physician that may pertain to that patient but is not instrumental in his management. Any correspondence between the physician and his malpractice insurance carrier would come under this heading and should be kept in a separate file. The most important items would be letters to the physician regarding any peer review action. Because it is part of the patient's record, even if the letter is favorable for the physician, it could be discoverable and, therefore, other aspects of the peer review could be discoverable as well. This type of "personal" correspondence belongs in a separate file.

If office personnel are allowed to make entries in the patient's record, the physician should have a policy established regarding who is allowed to make them, the content of these entries, and the routine for reviewing them. Consider the following interchange during a deposition.

> LAWYER: Tell me the procedure you go through and how these entries are made. How come part of this is your handwriting and part of it is the girl's handwriting?

> WITNESS: The part of the time the girl is there, part of the time she is probably preparing the other patients.

> LAWYER: So you just kind of comment to her and, say, the name of the girl in this case is who?

> WITNESS: As far as I can judge from this, it was Jane.

The inquisitor is asking a compound question with two distinct parts (see Chapter nine, *The inquisition*). The witness answered the second part of the question. An alternative way of answering could take the following form.

> LAWYER: Tell me the procedure by which you go and how these entries are made. How come part of this is your handwriting and part of it is the girl's handwriting?

WITNESS: Your question has two parts. Which part would you like me to answer first?

LAWYER: Why is part of this in the girl's handwriting?

WITNESS: The girl you refer to is Jane Doe who has authority and routinely makes such entries in my patients' records.

Typographical errors are fairly common in hospital dictations and need correction, but those corrections should be done when the physician is completing his signatures in the chart. Even we physicians occasionally dictate the wrong description. I recently saw a patient with a mammogram reporting an abnormality on the right side that the patient insisted was on the left. The patient turned out to be correct and the radiologist dictated an addendum to the report after reviewing the x-rays again.

Physicians are in the habit of quickly rummaging through incomplete hospital records to scribble their signatures in the appropriate blank spaces. The advent of computerized charting is making this task even quicker to complete. We intuitively feel that the record is for our use and for communication with other physicians, but we should take the time to be sure the dictation reads correctly. We never know when it will wind up in the hands of a lawyer bent on emptying our deep pockets.

Many years ago, a lawsuit against a surgeon was settled out of court because the patient claimed she had problems attributable to an anal sphincterotomy. The surgeon was well-trained and had a vast amount of rectal surgery experience. He knew the indications and technique for an internal anal sphincterotomy. However, in the body of his dictated operative note was the word "external". Even though this patient had an independent examiner report her sphincter tone was still present, the defense felt that a jury would be sympathetic to the patient if signed documentation showed the surgeon cut the wrong muscle. A correction of his inadvertent remark at the time he signed the report could have proven to be more defensible.

Timing of the documentation is important. We should dictate each operative report as soon as the case is completed, or at least before the day is done. An operative report dictated more than 24 hours after the procedure will be questioned. An attorney can use this delay to convince a judge or jury enough time passed so that the operator could not have remembered the exact details of the case.

I believe the days of a surgeon picking up a dictation phone and saying, "Please use my standard hysterectomy report," should be of historical significance only. I came across an operative report from a hospital back east while there consulting on a medical staff matter. In effect it read:

Doctor, you want us to use your standard dictation and we cannot find it in our file. Please re-dictate the report.

We can easily picture a plaintiff's lawyer asking a jury whether or not the surgeon was giving the patient his full attention if he perceived him as "standard". Care practices are standard, not patients.

Verbal orders to a nurse in person or by phone should be reviewed as well during the patient's hospitalization. We should refrain from giving orders verbally when we are standing on the patient's ward unless the chart is nowhere to be found. On occasion, a nurse will misunderstand a physician and write an order incorrectly. Co-signing an order written in error has the potential of opening a deep pocket.

Reviewing the available records

It is commonplace for a plaintiff's lawyer to ask the witness how he prepared for the deposition. The following is an example of such an inquiry.

> LAWYER: Have you done anything to prepare your-self for the deposition today?
>
> WITNESS: Yes.
>
> LAWYER: What?
>
> WITNESS: I reviewed the chart.
>
> LAWYER: When?
>
> WITNESS: This past week.
>
> LAWYER: Today is Friday, the 23rd. Was it within the last seven days?
>
> WITNESS: Yes.
>
> LAWYER: Was it over last weekend?
>
> WITNESS: No.
>
> LAWYER: When was it?
>
> WITNESS: I started reviewing it Monday.

In another instance a hospital technician is being deposed.

> LAWYER: Have you been able to do anything besides looking at the hospital record concerning the patient to

refresh your recollection at all concerning the events that occurred on that day or around that day of June 29th?

WITNESS: I just looked at the chart.

LAWYER: Is there anything else that is available to you that you know of that might assist you in recalling the specific circumstances surrounding the events of that day?

WITNESS: Not that I'm aware of.

Any physician or nurse involved in the care of a plaintiff should sit down and read every notation in the patient's chart. I realize that many charts are enormous, especially if the patient was hospitalized for weeks or months, but the witness should make every attempt to organize the chart in his or her mind. It would be ideal if we could memorize the entire chart, but this is not often possible.

What must be memorized are the locations of pertinent entries and basic content of those entries. There is also the ritual of putting aside any cloudy recollection of the case. Remember, not everything you recall right away may be accurate (see Chapter six, *Telling the truth*).

When organizing the chart and committing to memory the important entries, do not overlook the nurses' notes. A prominent attorney explained to me that these entries are the most important for him to read and the most helpful in finding the gems needed to support his case. Since lawyers frequently treat this part of the record like a Bible, it is important that we review these ourselves and know their basic content before testifying. It is vitally important to be prepared to discuss any discrepancies that may exist between your observations and the nurse's.

Several hundred thousand dollars changed hands in a settlement that might have been prevented had a nurse memorized her own notations in the hospital record.

LAWYER: How long was it from the time that you noted in your record that Dr. Jones stated the patient had a cardiac arrest until Dr. Smith arrived in the room?

WITNESS: I really don't recall how long it was.

LAWYER: Can you give me your best estimate by virtue of what you know happened from the time that Dr. Jones stated that the patient had a cardiac arrest until, the way you remember it, Dr. Smith and/or Dr. Brown came into the room?

WITNESS: It is very difficult for me to recall the amount of time it took. I don't recall.

LAWYER: Can you put it in any parameters at all? For example, can you say it was greater or less than ten minutes?

WITNESS: My impression is that it must have been about 10 minutes, maybe 15.

The nurse clearly documented in her note that the doctors "arrived immediately". The lawyer in this case gave her a clue at the beginning of this phase of questioning: "How long was it from the time that *you noted in your record*...". Had she memorized her note, the dialogue could have appeared differently.

LAWYER: How long was it from the time that you noted in your record that Dr. Jones stated the patient had a cardiac arrest until Dr. Smith arrived in the room?

WITNESS: According to my note, the doctors arrived immediately.

LAWYER: Can you give me your best estimate by virtue of what you know happened from the time that Dr. Jones stated that the patient had a cardiac arrest until, the way you remember it, Dr. Smith and/or Dr. Brown came into the room?

WITNESS: I don't recall exactly. I know they arrived immediately.

LAWYER: Can you put it in any parameters at all? For example, can you say it was greater or less than ten minutes?

WITNESS: I can only say they arrived immediately.

Since the basis for this lawsuit was a supposed delay in treatment until the doctors arrived, the outcome of the case could have been much different if the nurse had answered the questions based upon her own documentation.

Detailed nursing documentation may be another argument in favor of exclusion flow sheets. Many hospitals are developing policies of less writing for the nursing staff to provide more patient care time. The downside of this is the increased amount of actual paperwork. In some instances, a separate chart is seen sitting next to the regular patient chart. This extra paper is necessary to fulfill the time-honored requirement of having everything written down. If it isn't documented, it didn't happen. Omissions of data provide fuel for the litigant's fire.

When the drive toward electronic charting becomes universal, I will be interested in how lawyers will attempt to distort the data. I fear the only advantage to such modern technology will be the preservation of our forests.

After careful review of all medical records available to you, it's time to review any depositions that have already taken place. Your lawyer should provide you with these. As mentioned above, knowing what another party did or did not testify to will come in handy when the plaintiff's lawyer or other defense counsel try to elaborate on someone's else testimony (see Chapter nine, *The inquisition*).

After review of the written materials available, it is often helpful to sit down with a blank piece of paper and make a flow sheet for your own personal use. Your counsel may also ask that you complete a form such as the one developed by Attorney Douglas Danner. Filling in the blanks gives the physician defendant a clearer idea of the hurdles his or her lawyer has to overcome.

Using a timeline format you can recreate the sequence of events, paying careful attention to dates and pertinent facts as well as making notations of locations of data and comments by other witnesses. Then memorize your flow sheet. It is unwise to bring any documents you have used for preparation to your deposition since any material present may be obtained by the plaintiff's lawyer and used accordingly.

I learned the importance of this intense study approach from my own experience. Several years ago, I was deposed in a malpractice complaint. I had not been sued, but my name was on the chart as a witness to an event. Following my own advice, I spent many hours studying the chart and memorizing the pertinent entries as well as reviewing other depositions. My labor paid off.

> LAWYER: Let me ask you to assume it to be true that Dr. Jones has testified under oath in this case that from the time the cardiac arrest was announced by Dr. Smith until there was a return of normal spontaneous cardiac activity, he was never able to appreciate a pulse. Do you have any reason, any facts to disagree with his testimony?

At this point, I carefully repeated the question to myself. After all, there was no stopwatch governing my answer. The word "pulse" stood out. I recalled seeing a dictation mentioning the pulse. Then I broke one of my own rules; I shared my thoughts out loud. The lawyer, frustrated with me, responded promptly.

> WITNESS: He may have been talking about a pulse without CPR.
>
> LAWYER: I want you to assume it to be true that he indicated he was never able to appreciate a pulse. Do you have any reason, any facts that are available to you to indicate that was not the situation that existed at that time?
>
> WITNESS: May I have a minute?

I knew that Dr. Jones had never testified to that effect in his deposition since I reviewed it carefully. I also recalled Dr. Jones mentioned the word "pulse" in a dictation. Quickly reviewing his dictations in the patient's chart, I found exactly what I was looking for.

> WITNESS: In Dr. Jones' Op note, he says the aorta was palpated, and there was no evidence of any return of the pulse when Dr. Brown stopped the cardiac massage.

The lawyer had intentionally given me information that was untrue and wanted me to verify it (see Chapter nine, *The inquisition*) to support his effort in convincing a jury that the patient was lying on the table for an inordinately long time without a pulse of any kind. I was able to alter his premise with documentation supporting the presence of a pulse with CPR.

No one can be expected to memorize every single word in the chart or other depositions, but organizing the information in such a way that you know exactly where to find information will help to alleviate confusion during the interrogation process.

Reviewing the literature

Medical personnel, especially physicians, must understand that we have a positive role to play in malpractice litigation in doing our own homework and in educating counsel. Our defense lawyers need help in locating pertinent medical articles as well as finding the proper textbooks. Occasionally this literature search will have already taken place to answer questions in the plaintiff lawyer's interrogatories which are usually completed months before a deposition takes place.

The Boy Scout Rule applies here as well. The inquisitor may want to know just how much you know about a specific subject. He or she has every right to ask these questions if that specific subject was an issue when you were involved in the patient's care. Careful review of current literature will prepare you to meet this challenge, even if it only turns out to be an intellectual exercise.

The lawyer will want to convince a jury that his client's problem is clearly due to negligence or gross deviation in standard of care because no other patient has ever had a similar outcome. To dispel this premise, do your homework. During the same deposition mentioned earlier, I was asked the following question.

> LAWYER: Do you know of a single case of reported anoxic encephalopathy that has occurred within such a brief period of anoxia?
>
> WITNESS: In doing research, trying to find out the possible causes of this patient's arrest, I came across a chapter where the author lists cardiac arrests and what they were due to, and it seems to me that there were a couple of cases mentioned where the standard of care was met and proper monitoring was done and the patient was resuscitated quickly and still died, either immediately or in a couple of days, from cerebral edema.

I didn't follow my own rules very well. In the first place, he asked me a question that could have been answered with a simple "yes". Second, if he then wanted more information, I could have simply referred him to the source.

In many cases, there is a preponderance of material available to support the care given. In sentinel events of a more unusual nature, spending time doing a thorough computer literature search may be necessary.

The rehearsal

If your lawyer does not offer to spend time with you, demand that he do so or contact your malpractice carrier. I am often amazed how little potential witnesses have been briefed by their own lawyers when we sit down for a practice session.

Practice should consist of learning how to recognize the various forms of questions (see Chapter nine, *The inquisition*). The more innocent a physician feels, the quicker he will want to offer the answers as well as more information than is required at the time. The lawyer should work diligently with the witness to curtail divulging any unnecessary details when answering.

The pattern of questioning by the lawyers can be examined from previous depositions. If there are areas a lawyer will tend to focus on, it is wise to be prepared to answer similar questions, especially if these areas are within the realm of your expected expertise.

This is also the time for your counsel to explain the meaning of objections by him or other lawyers at the deposition (see Chapter eleven, *General advice*). He should also review with you what is considered privileged information and the purpose of off-the-record conversations. You should also be counseled in how to deal with the lawyer who becomes irritated or just plain rude (see Chapter ten, *Traps to avoid*).

A good rehearsal is as important for a physician's medical malpractice deposition as it is for a performer's opening night on Broadway.

Opening night and the 15% rule

Despite the care with which some people have done their homework, there is still the *probability*, not *possibility*, that the witness will feel stumped by a question or two. This is because he or she may be experiencing opening night jitters, a phenomenon common to performers.

Even the most seasoned entertainers will feel butterflies when performing a new routine. During my younger days as a violinist, an orchestra conductor explained to me that we should practice intending to reach 115% perfection because on stage we risk losing fifteen percent.

I was enjoying a figure skating exhibition on television one evening when an Olympic medalist stopped her performance for a few seconds and just stroked around the ice. She then picked up the routine and brought it to a flawless finish. During an interview after the show, she remarked that she didn't know what happened. Her mind suddenly went blank. She was a victim of the fifteen percent loss.

The following example comes early in a physician's deposition.

> LAWYER: So, when did you come back to Anytown?
>
> WITNESS: I believe '91. Yes.
>
> LAWYER: January of '91?
>
> WITNESS: I can't tell you exactly.
>
> LAWYER: Give us your best feel for it.
>
> WITNESS: I don't want to.
>
> LAWYER: Why is that?
>
> WITNESS: Because I can't give you the exact answer, and if I can't give you the exact answer, I would just rather not give you one because I want to make sure I give you correct answers.

For the record, this particular physician is a well-trained specialist who had attended one of my seminars. He was obviously concerned about giving accurate answers, and he was right in being so (see Chapter six, *Telling the truth*). I would venture to say that most of us remember the month and maybe even the day we began practice. However, our witness here can't recall the month he returned to town. He was demonstrating the fifteen percent performance loss.

Another example.

> LAWYER: Did you during the time you treated Susie have contact with her mother also?
>
> WITNESS: Yes, sir.
>
> LAWYER: And would you know her mother, do you think, if she walked in?
>
> WITNESS: Yes, sir.
>
> LAWYER: Do you recall her mother's first name?
>
> WITNESS: Yes, I know it. I know her last name is Lopez.
>
> LAWYER: This isn't a guessing game. I just wanted to see if you knew. Her name is Anna, I believe?
>
> WITNESS: Yes, it just left my mind.

Any other time, I'm sure our doctor would remember the mother's name, but her mind was occupied with more important details. Fortunately, she had prepared so well for this encounter, the fifteen percent loss was relatively unimportant.

Summary

- Even if you are not being sued, prepare for the deposition as if you are.
- Remember that your own documentation offers the best clues to what actually happened.
- Commit to memory as much of the chart and other records as possible, paying special attention to the location of information in the various sections.
- Review any other depositions and be familiar with the testimony.
- Review all the literature you can find pertinent to the case or the main sources if the care in question is relatively common.
- Be prepared to explain any discrepancies in documentation or any duplication of reports.

- Know your material to 115% accuracy. Remember, it's your Opening Night and the 15% loss in performance.
- Sit down with your lawyer and discuss the different areas upon which the inquisitor may focus and the various types of questions he may ask.

Even the most proficient witness will not give a perfect performance, but he can be prepared well enough that any loss of information will not support an unjustified outcome in the case.

References

Blumenkopf, J. S., Deposition strategy and tactics, *American Journal of Trial Advocacy Special*, 1987.

Brallier, J. M., *Lawyers and Other Reptiles*, Contemporary Books, 1992.

Danner, D., *Medical Malpractice, A Primer for Physicians*, Lawyers Cooperative Publishing Company, 1985.

Hirsch, B., Preparing a med mal case, *Lawyers Weekly USA*, Sept. 25, 1995.

Keeton, R. E., *Trial Tactics & Methods*, Little Brown & Company, 1973.

Mutual Insurance Company of Arizona, Documentation: Sword or Shield, Audiotape, 1998.

Nora, P. F., *Professional Liability/Risk Management*, American College of Surgeons, 1997.

chapter eight

Meeting the inquisitor

"No brilliance is needed in the law. Nothing but common sense, and relatively clean fingernails."

John Mortimer

A deposition is not just a record for the court. It is also an opportunity for the plaintiff's counsel to size up the defendant. The lawyer will be interested in how the doctor dresses, his physical appearance, his presence, his demeanor, and his mannerisms. In addition to giving the lawyer a chance to find out how effectively the doctor's testimony will benefit the plaintiff's position, it also gives him or her an overview of the defendant's credibility. Even though the witness is not answering questions directly to an audience of jurors, the plaintiff's lawyer will still be able to glean an idea of how he will come across in an open courtroom.

From the witness's standpoint the only purpose of the deposition is to document the truth in writing for the court. Any inherent gift for persuasion can be left at home since influencing the jury is not the goal of this particular part of the discovery process. Convincing a jury of your innocence is best done in person and that should be left for trial.

The first key to success has already been addressed — thorough preparation. If a witness walks into the room feeling that the lawyer or lawyers will eat him alive, that is exactly what will happen. The theory of the self-fulfilling prophecy can play a devastating role in the malpractice deposition if the witness is unprepared. How the witness will perform depends on how he *believes* he will perform; he cannot outperform his own expectations.

The witness now must approach his inquisitor with the right amount of confidence, not too much nor too little. The purpose of the encounter is not to win the case but merely to add a major piece of evidence. If the witness remembers that the cards are stacked in his favor because he has more knowledge about the facts surrounding the issue than the lawyer, he can walk into the arena with poise and assurance.

Credibility as well as powers of persuasion are directly proportional to the physical attractiveness of the person in question. Good-looking people, especially men, are perceived as being intelligent and successful while stunning beauty in women may actually work against their credibility. Fame itself imparts attractiveness. Celebrities can possess tremendous powers of influence despite less-than-perfect physical features. Each witness must evaluate his individual physical characteristics and make every effort to present himself exactly as he wants the public to see him.

The question of having the wrong hairstyle, being too fat or too skinny, having too big a nose, etc. is more of an issue when the defendant actually has to face the jury, and is a subject for another book. The deposition is an isolated instance in which the witness only has to present himself to the plaintiff's lawyer and other defense attorneys. He will still be sized up by those lawyers as to what potential effect the witness may have on a jury.

The Chanel rule

I am often asked how one should dress for his or her initial interrogation. The fact is that it doesn't matter except insofar as the deposition is an opportunity for the plaintiff's lawyer to see the witness, especially a defendant. Actually, the old saying "clothes make the man" bears some weight when it comes to initial impressions.

We subconsciously size up strangers within the first six or seven seconds of meeting. Keeping that in mind, the way we extend our hand, our eye contact, the tone of our voice, etc. all have a part in forming an immediate impression on the person we're facing for the first time. That is why celebrities take so much care in their physical appearance; the public is sure to notice them, and the only impression most people will take home with them is what they *see*.

Appearance is everything, but it has several components, some of which we can control and some we cannot. A red-headed woman entering a room will engrave a decidedly different impression in the minds of those present than will a blond. The same is true for the length of the woman's hair. A short hairstyle that has been hailed as cute by girlfriends may appear threatening to a group of men. Likewise, tall stature commands more respect than short. A man entering a room sporting long hair and a motorcycle jacket will not be instantaneously filed in our subconscious along with corporate CEOs we've met wearing Brooks Brothers suits.

We have no control over our ethnic background and our dress can tell a lot about us. I recall a story about a physician who was born in New York to a couple from India. He was of Sikh heritage and wore his turban with pride.

The doctor was enjoying the presentation of a guest lecturer, a nematologist, one evening. The speaker was describing a particularly nasty specimen when he parenthetically commented to the physician in the audience, "We don't see these much in this country, but I bet you see them in your home." "Nope," the doctor replied, "We don't see too many of those in Flatbush."

A witness may be proud of the culture he has inherited, but it may not be viewed with the same adoration by a jury. I recall an instance in which a juror remarked that the defendant physician who immigrated to this country could have prevented the patient's misfortune by simply staying in his homeland.·

On one occasion, I deliberately chose a pink-flowered cotton dress with a white lace collar for a deposition hoping the plaintiff's attorney would be tempted to begin gently with his interrogation. I sat quietly in my seat opposite the lawyer with my hands folded in my lap. I was anxious to see if it affected his initial perception of me, and my suspicions were confirmed.

While setting up for the interrogation, one of the parties opened a closet saying, "The only thing here is a shotgun." The plaintiff's lawyer quipped, "Great. We've had enough threats against us in this case already." Not missing a beat I added in my best I'm-going-to-get-you-for-this voice, "Obviously none serious enough."

The lawyer's jaw dropped. He pulled himself back in his chair, adjusted his coat and leaned forward in preparation for battle. My flippant remark blew my cover. He knew his opponent was not what she seemed, and the time spent ironing the cotton dress had been wasted.

Not long ago I was called to assist in preparing a female physician for a malpractice trial. When first contacted, I responded with an audible moan. She was not endowed with physical traits our culture considers desirable and she was moderately overweight. The first thing I had to do was take her shopping. Neither the trial nor my service ever came to pass as the insurance company settled shortly thereafter.

Her deposition was history, but I knew that her initial impression on the plaintiff's attorney and the other attorneys involved in this case was not as favorable as it could have been. Everyone has characteristics that are more pleasing or more positive than others, and enhancing these from the beginning could have helped emphasize the fact that she was a competent physician.

Business executives are aware of the importance of first impressions. I asked a CEO from California if he had ever been to my neck of the woods. He answered affirmatively, but remarked that he was reluctant to come back to Yuma because, during his last visit, he was detained at the Mexican border while trying to re-enter the United States. "They thought I was a drug dealer," he explained. "I'm dark-complected and I guess I look like a criminal." He was absolutely right. Dressed in an expensive, well-tailored suit, this man gave the appearance of a high-class movie villain. In reality, he was an honest, law-abiding citizen who ran a successful, legitimate business.

Our outer covering, our veneer, is all that will be perceived during our encounters with malpractice lawyers whether in the deposition or in the courtroom. Neither occasion will give anyone the opportunity to learn what the witness is really like. Therefore, the witness must make sure he comes across favorably.

While there are no rules governing our physical appearance at a deposition, we leave an indelible mark on all those present. Think of walking into the room wearing a designer tennis outfit and laying the keys to your Jaguar on the table in front of the plaintiff's lawyer. It might leave a lasting impression that could come back to haunt you in front of a jury.

Lawyers will gladly accommodate an overweight witness at deposition. Obesity fosters negative responses, especially in a jury. The actual condition of being overweight may be perceived as a character flaw since no one in his right mind would want to be fat.

I propose *The Chanel Rule*: whether it is a deposition or a trial, make every effort to present yourself as you want to be seen by others, but be comfortable enough that your appearance does not make you feel self-conscious and does not detract from your testimony. It is known that physically attractive people automatically have more credibility, but don't overdo it especially if it makes you feel awkward.

Lawyers know all the tricks. This is why defendants accused of homicide and other major crimes are almost always seen clean-shaven, well-coiffed, and neatly dressed. A lawyer may even suggest a client wear a wedding band to convey a more stable lifestyle. If the client is male, the lawyer will probably suggest leaving the earring at home. Any piece of jewelry that could be construed as body piercing should not be visible and the same holds true for tattoos.

Even masters at the art of jury illusion will occasionally fail. I watched a video testimony given by a CEO of a major corporation. I'm sure his lawyer coached him on his dress and manner, yet I don't believe he was served well by the advice. The jury, knowing this man headed a mega-business, was looking at a witness dressed in a drab suit and tie that could have been purchased at a factory outlet for a major discount store. He was sitting on the stand with both hands between his knees, slumped over the microphone answering most of the questions with his eyes directed downward, the same direction his credibility was headed.

I believe the attorney for this CEO wanted to give the jury the impression that his client was a down-to-earth fellow who did not differ from them in any way, but the jury didn't buy it. They knew how a CEO should present himself.

Another witness in a videotaped trial was a young adult male. He was a husky fellow who obviously spent a lot of time in the gym. He wore a thick sweater which emphasized his build and he sat on the stand leaning slightly forward with his arms resting on the arms of the chair. It was clear that he was attentive to the questioning and had nothing to hide. It was difficult to tell whether or not he had completed high school, but that didn't matter. He came across exactly as he wanted others to see him. This man would have surely lost every ounce of credibility had his lawyer dressed him in an Armani suit.

The atmosphere in any legal arena, deposition or courtroom, is scary enough without worrying about binding garments or whether or not every hair is in place. Since the vast majority of physicians and other medical personnel called to deposition or trial are innocent of wrong-doing, the focus should be on building confidence in the testimony and credibility in presentation.

Lawyers and jurors expect physicians to be successful financially. The trend is going in the other direction with the dwindling reimbursements, but the current perception by the public is unchanged. We are expected to dress well, but not too well. Be yourself and be comfortable, but ask your lawyer or your friends for suggestions if you are concerned that you may be giving the wrong initial impression to either the lawyers or a jury. Assuming that we are *looking* our best, we can move on to our behavior during a deposition.

Lights! Camera! Inaction!

The jury will never see the way the witness was dressed during the deposition. Likewise, the body language, tone of voice, or mannerisms will be a mystery as well unless the jury is exposed to a videotaped presentation. If a witness will be unavailable for trial or the lawyer does not want to shell out the money for travel expenses, this visual form of evidence, while acceptable to the court, can shed a different light on deposition testimony.

Just as people vary in their physical attractiveness, we also have different degrees of photogenicity. The art of perception has been taken to new heights by photographers and make-up artists in the motion picture and advertising industries. With the right lighting and other accoutrements, anyone can be made attractive, sensuous, commanding, or even evil. Unfortunately, a deposition recorded on film puts emphasis only on the identification of the witness and the spoken word, and the witness will frequently come across as if he is in a line-up.

We all have a good side, facially speaking. The human face is not symmetrical and a few moments with your computer and scanner can demonstrate this. Using a full-face photograph, you can either fold or cut the photo in half down the middle of the long axis. Piecing two right halves together and two left halves together reveals basically the same person but with two different attitudes or emotions represented. Also, transposing the right side of the face for the left gives a slightly different look to the same person.

Many of us know which is our best side, but we rarely have control over the physical layout of a video deposition. If you know your left side shows emotional changes more than the right, you might consider asking the camera operator to shoot from your right side since maintaining an even calm is more crucial in the filmed setting.

A witness rarely looks good giving filmed testimony. The light is frequently from the ambient source or the operator might select a one-directional soft light or straight hard light. All of these choices serve only to enhance the character and emotions of the subject.

Fluorescent light can be unflattering since it will make the eye sockets appear darker and, hence, give a harsh appearance to the subject. One method used to soften the eyes and other facial features is wearing a light color such as white or cream under the face to mute the stark effect. A white shirt or blouse will serve this purpose nicely, but spreading the white copies of a chart or other pieces of evidence on the table directly in front of the witness can have a similar effect.

Attorneys know the power of video in front of a jury and will use such an opportunity to its fullest. The witness should be wary of the inquisitor who moves around the room during his questioning. Such activity causes the witness to follow with his eyes, and this type of movement may appear shifty to the jurors. Subtleties in expression and body language are far more important in this setting. Even though video is rarely used in defendant depositions for medical malpractice, the witness should be alert to its potential jury effect.

My place or yours?

The location of the deposition is of importance only insofar as it should not be on the witness's property. Physicians especially will agree to being deposed in their offices, thinking of the convenience afforded them, but this can be even more convenient for the lawyer. It gives the opposition an opportunity to see how the doctor lives, what books he keeps in his library, what certificates are hanging on the wall, what his office personnel are like, and how he handles interruptions.

The deposition should be done on neutral territory and at a time when the witness will be able to devote his full attention to the ordeal without unnecessary interruptions. Answering your beeper or phone during a deposition only delays the inevitable, and the lawyer can ask to suspend that meeting and reschedule the taking of your testimony. It is best to check out to a colleague and put your life on hold until the deposition has been completed. Any efforts to sabotage the lawyer's efforts at deposing you will only be viewed unfavorably by the courts.

Body language

A seasoned malpractice lawyer will smell fear across the table. An angry or nervous witness is guaranteed to make a mistake during the interrogation. Aggressive behavior in this setting is usually a sign of low self-esteem and a feeling of being trapped. A physician who shows his insecurity will be putty in the hands of a clever plaintiff lawyer.

That doesn't mean that he should be cocky and overly confident; the lawyer will destroy that attitude halfway through the ordeal. The same demeanor you have when you walk into the room is the same demeanor you should have when you leave. You are not there to make friends. You are there merely to answer questions.

Begin your preparation by soaking in a warm bath. This will help to relax the skeletal musculature and dilate the subpapillary plexus of the skin giving a warm and tingling feeling. The end result will be a decrease in your general neural-firing rate and an elevation of your fear activation threshold, making it more difficult for your body to sense anxiety.

Dine on light nourishment before going to the deposition. This will allow you to complete the interrogation without your stomach making "feed me" noises. Fish has been purported to sharpen the mind and enhance recall, while a diet high in fats and carbohydrates may weigh you down. Do not eat as if it is your last meal.

The plaintiff's attorney is the enemy, but common courtesy dictates that you be civil in your approach to meeting him; that doesn't mean you have to shake his hand. A simple nod when he is introduced to you will suffice. Be cool but not aloof. Be confident but not overpowering. There is no way in the world you will win his friendship or even respect nor will you or your care for the patient be vindicated during the deposition. You must simply show the opposition that you will be formidable competition in the upcoming events.

Most of us were probably in grade school when we first learned about the concept of body language and the messages we silently send to others. We all know that crouching up into a ball tells those around us that we want to withdraw and hide. Even crossing our legs in a direction away from someone can be interpreted as a desire to be elsewhere. Folding our arms is also viewed as a defensive move.

My advice for the witness differs depending on whether we are dealing with a deposition or a trial. The same mannerisms appropriate at the initial inquisition may be viewed differently by a jury in a courtroom. It is my intention to limit discussion in this book to techniques that may be useful in the deposition setting.

The witness should enter the room early if possible. That will give him a chance to select a choice seat. Leaders, like heads of families, will pick a place at the head of the table. This is not necessarily the optimal position during the deposition. The court reporter will frequently occupy that seat.

It is convenient for the lawyer running the deposition to sit directly across from the witness with the other attorneys taking the remaining seats around the table. A witness may, however, consider taking a seat in the middle of the table or at least one seat away with his own attorney sitting next to the court reporter. This will give the witness access to his lawyer without having to turn his head away from the inquisitor.

A position in the center of the table also affords a certain amount of control over the proceedings. It gives the witness easy access to all documents lying on the table as well as the other people present during the deposition. I also try to choose a seat in which I am not sitting with my back to the door. That way I can see whoever comes and goes and I have a good view of all the activity.

The fewer moves used finding and taking your seat, the more confident you will appear to others present. Females are noted for using four times the number of motions actually necessary to enter a room, pull out a chair, and get comfortable. Males, on the other hand, will usually enter a room and find a seat with very few different body moves.

If you are sitting in a position of control, you will be less likely to experience anxiety during the proceedings even though you will not be doing most of the talking. Many witnesses approach a deposition with trepidation simply because they do not realize they are holding in their minds and records the information the lawyer is itching to obtain. A witness is, by virtue of his wealth of knowledge, in control.

Making yourself at home is the next move. A witness can mark his new territory much as a dog does when moving into a new home. For those readers with an active imagination, the similarity ends with the analogy. If you are carrying your keys, a box of tissues, or anything else you may need during the deposition, lay them out on the table to mark your boundaries. This will serve as a silent message to the others present and it is doubtful that anyone will invade your space.

Be sure you have a glass of water in front of you and easy access to more. Talking, especially in a potentially stressful situation, will lead to a cotton mouth. Check the temperature of the room and make sure it is suitable for *your* comfort. Being the witness gives you a built-in advantage for controlling the environment in which you must perform. The plaintiff's attorney will often ask if there are any changes that need to be made before you begin testifying. Also, you do not have to tolerate interruptions or annoying distractions such as noises from another room, talking, or music.

Witnesses are often told they may walk around the room while answering the questions or they may take frequent breaks. Make every effort to sit quietly throughout the questioning. However, if physical limitations such as recent orthopedic surgery or neural compression necessitates mobility, it is best to mention this early in the proceeding.

The human brain functions best with rest periods at 90-minute intervals. When working on a major project or studying for an exam, cerebral saturation peaks at about 90 minutes and a break after that period of time is warranted.

It is probably more effective to keep your hands in plain sight. Folding them in your lap only offers temptation to fidget if confronted with a difficult question. Also, by showing your hands, you are laying your cards on the table, so to speak, and clearly have nothing to hide. It is also less awkward when you need to reach for the chart or examine other exhibits.

If you have any nervous ticks, leave them home. Even though this is much more important in a courtroom setting, the lawyer will still be watching to see how you might appear to the jury. Repeated scratching of the nose, rubbing the earlobe, twisting the hair, and other superfluous activity should be avoided.

The most common nervous habits I have seen during interrogation are the bouncing leg and the thumping pencil, and the witnesses were completely unaware of these activities. If you wonder whether or not you have any such mannerisms, it is best to ask family members or friends before entering your deposition.

A doctor was complaining to me that he wasn't going to change any of his mannerisms or alter his approach to the plaintiff's lawyer because, as he explained, it was *dishonest*. I responded with the question, "Do you truly believe you are innocent of any neglect or wrong-doing in this case?" He nodded. "Then is presenting yourself in such a way as to drill that message into the lawyers *dishonest*?" Just as we look for the common denominator in the standard of care, we must achieve a similar common denominator when it comes to convincing others of our credibility.

Listening with the eyes

Our communication skills tell a lot about us. A physician can be the most brilliant in the world and yet he can fail miserably in a question and answer session such as our court system has devised. Outside the medical field, it is not uncommon for the inferior of two employees to be granted a promotion and, more often than not, the decision will be based on that person's greater talent as a communicator. The witness in a deposition will be worthless if he is unable to express himself effectively and get the truth documented for the court to see.

How you deliver your answers during the deposition is not as critical as how the answers are transcribed for the court. All the answers could be given in a monotone and the judge and jury would never know the difference. Still, the witness would be wise to use the same steady, low-pitched voice he would use if counseling a patient. The words should be delivered clearly and at an appropriate speed, not too fast nor too slow, so that the reporter can catch every word.

The use of filler expressions and noises must be avoided. Remarks such as "yeah," "let's see," "you know," and "let me think," do not add to the witness's credibility at all. Likewise, beginning an answer with "It seems to me" or "I think" limits the facts to your own personal experience or opinion. Any answer that is prefaced with "I'm not too sure," or "I'm only guessing" should be answered simply as "I don't know."

The use of the word "but" is important in depositions because it annuls everything before it. If you find yourself tempted to use "but" at the end of a clause, try to put a period instead and start the next sentence with the information coming after the "but."

Copying the lawyer's rate of speech, intensity, and pitch serves no purpose in a deposition setting and can, in fact, make the witness look as foolish or insecure as the lawyer. Avoidance of this type of interspeaker influence is recommended; try not to copy the lawyer's speech pattern or mannerisms as they are not necessarily indicative of his true thoughts.

Showing an intense interest in the proceedings is a hallmark of attorney behavior during a deposition. He will frequently have a portfolio chocked full of notes and exhibits, many of which will be stacked on the table in plain sight. The rate at which the lawyer refers to his notes is directly proportional to the effectiveness of the witness. If the questions suddenly appear to flow like wine, it is usually due to new evidence presented by the witness and this can lead to a whole new line of questioning. A lawyer who refers to his notes frequently and takes long pauses is either unprepared or has failed to elicit the answers he desired.

The lawyer may take on a poker face, occasionally accompanied by a sheepish grin. He may sit back in his chair directing the questions to an imaginary witness on the ceiling or he might stare intently into the witness's eyes with a perpetually amazed look on his face with every answer. He may even lean over the desk almost invading the witness's space or speak in a loud voice as if the witness were deaf. All of these forms of behavior should be ignored by the witness in favor of devoting full attention to the actual question.

The lawyer will be hanging onto our every word, but he will also be sizing up how our responses are presented. If the witness answers in a forthright manner with a voice that exudes confidence, the lawyer will evaluate that voice's power of seduction over a jury.

The lawyer will not only listen with his ears, but also with his eyes. Expressions and motions used while answering a question as well as those observed during the asking of that question will be closely monitored. Biting the lower lip, taking a deep breath, or pushing away from the table during a question will send a message to the lawyer that he has touched a sensitive area.

Human nature dictates our response to feedback. I was giving a lecture to a group of physicians, several of whom were from a highly prestigious medical center. They sat with their arms folded looking at me with a flat affect, unlike the other participants who were showing more interest. In response to the exclusive clique of doctors, I interrupted my talk and said, "I bet you're wondering what a surgeon from Yuma can possibly teach you." In unison, they nodded. After a brief discussion, they relaxed and we had meaningful exchanges throughout the rest of the day.

If a lawyer nods or smiles when the answers are given, the witness may subconsciously perceive this as confirmation of a good performance. When we have encouragement to talk, we usually talk more and that is exactly what the lawyer wants the witness to do, since a gabby witness can do a major part of the lawyer's work for him. The more verbiage, the better to eat you with, my dear.

In general, it is best to ignore any of the lawyer's gestures. They can be as dishonest and contrived as some of the questions he may ask (see Chapter nine, *The inquisition*).

More important are the witness's mannerisms and gestures in response to the questions. Awareness of how we process information cannot only improve our testimony posture but enhance our memory acquisition as well.

Lawyers and judges learn about what neurologists call *lateral eye movements* which are more familiar to students of Neurolinguistic Programming

(NLP) as *eye accessing cues*. We tell each other how we process information and divulge where many memories are stored in our cerebral data banks. The type of information processing is felt to be expressed in our eye movements.

While these concepts are still in the theoretical stage and there is a paucity of scientific research supporting them, they complement the theories of visual, auditory, and kinesthetic learning. NLP focuses on the direction of eye movement. If a piece of information was obtained visually (i.e., reading a report), accessing that information is done by directing the eyes upward and to the left in a right-handed individual and upward toward the right in a south paw.

Just as significant is the tendency to direct the eyes upward in the opposite direction if the person is trying to envision something he has never seen before. This might be observed in a witness who is trying to conjure up an answer about which he has no knowledge.

General events whether real or imagined may be accessed by unfocusing the eyes staring into space. This action can be practiced looking at stereograms: those pictures made up of repeated patterns that have hidden pictures within them. Bringing the concealed picture into focus is much the same as seeing the details surrounding an event we have not thought about for a long time.

Auditory processing is reflected by keeping the eyes central but glancing left or right depending upon whether the sounds were actual or imaginary. This activity can be seen in response to questions such as "What did the patient tell you?" or "What exactly was discussed at that meeting?"

These cues vary from one person to another but a single individual will usually be consistent in lateral eye movements. Much of our eye activity is culturally based, but people raised in the United States have a tendency to look at a person who is asking a question and avert their eyes to contemplate the answer.

Therefore, deliberately avoiding all eye contact will be viewed negatively in our society. It not only reflects a lack of respect for the speaker but also a lack of interest or self-confidence on the part of the listener. During a deposition we do not need to overtly demonstrate respect for our inquisitor, but we must look attentive.

The lawyer will observe the witness to see how he processes the questions. The witness would do well to be more conscious of the possible connection between eye movement and memory. A conversation might be more easily recalled in a right-handed witness by keeping the eyes central and glancing left, and visual recall may be enhanced by directing the eyes upward to the left.

Both the lawyer and the witness will be tempted to look away when processing more complicated ideas. This helps by decreasing the amount of external stimuli entering our brain. The same action will occur when the answer is not on the tip of our tongues. This type of visual diversion is common and expected when the subject at hand calls for details.

The witness must avoid looking all over the room or keeping a downward gaze as this may give the impression of discomfort or disinterest. A witness who is able to convince the lawyer he is processing the questions and delivering the correct answers could be that lawyer's worst nightmare.

People will also respond to questions differently depending upon the neuro-accessing system involved. A person thinking *visually* will have a tendency to speak more rapidly than one thinking through his auditory channels. A visual thinker's breathing will be more shallow and emanate from higher in the chest. Kinesthetic people will typically speak slowly with long pauses and breathe with their bellies.

Since most animals use their abdominal muscles to breathe, it stands to reason that man would do the same. Instead, we are coached from birth to "suck it in" and this forces us to be chest breathers expending more energy and requiring more conscious effort. In an attempt to make the best of a deposition situation, we should simply relax and breathe with our bellies.

Summary

The deposition gives the plaintiff's lawyer as well as all defense counsel present a chance to size up the witness. Since the witness's job is only to provide answers to questions, his demeanor is of less importance in deposition than in trial, but the delivery of those answers can tell the lawyers how comfortable the witness is with the case and how the witness prefers to process the information stored in his brain.

When you appear for the deposition you should:

- Take a warm bath before you go and eat a light meal.
- Dress neatly and comfortably, but not too casually.
- Arrive early and pick a seat.
- Sit down and shut up until you have been sworn in, i.e., do not chat with the lawyers.
- Mark your territory so that there is ample room to put your hands and review records.
- Beware of video cameras.
- Pour yourself a glass of water.
- Ignore the inquisitor's gestures, tone of voice, and facial expressions at all times.
- Try not to fidget.
- Look at the lawyer when he is asking a question even though he may not be looking at you.
- If you need to think about an answer, look away.
- If you are right-handed, look up and to the left to tap your visual memory bank.
- If the question deals with auditory information, look toward your left ear for the answer.
- Speak at a comfortable rate as if you are trying to explain something to a child.

- Use a soft but audible voice of moderate or low pitch with the normal inflections.
- If 90 minutes have passed and you have not had a break, ask for one.
- Breathe with your belly.

Familiarity with a particular situation breeds comfort and confidence. The more you testify in a deposition setting, the easier it is to walk in, sit down, and make the place your home for the next few hours even if the decorator was Edgar Allen Poe. Your attitude can help create a less stressful environment and, in turn, the inquisitor will perceive you to be a more relaxed witness.

The above suggestions are offered to help the witness appear cool and calm during the deposition. A confident witness is an effective witness whether it is at deposition or trial.

References

Andreas, S. and Faulkner, C., *NLP: The New Technology of Achievement*, William Morrow, 1994.

Brallier, J. M., *Lawyers and Other Reptiles*, Contemporary Books, 1992.

Childress, C. W., *Persuasive Delivery in the Courtroom*, Lawyers Cooperative Publishing, 1995.

Ekman, P., *Emotion in the Human Face*, Cambridge University Press, 1982.

Kennan, D., Deposing the defendant doctor: Preparation is crucial, *Trial*, 26, 69, 1990.

Knapp, M. L. and Hall, J. A., *Nonverbal Communication In Human Interaction*, Harcourt Brace College Publishers, 1992.

O'Connor, J. and Seymour, J., *Introducing NLP — Neuro-Linguistic Programming*, Thorsons, 1995.

chapter nine

The inquisition

In the fell clutch of circumstance
I have not winced nor cried aloud.
Under the bludgeonings of chance
my head is bloody, but unbowed.

William Ernest Henley
from *Invictus*

A physician defendant was sitting across from a plaintiff's lawyer. Ninety minutes into the questioning, the following exchange occurred.

LAWYER: Is it your position, Doctor, that your treatment of Mrs. Ketchum was in keeping within the standard of care for a lady with her condition?

WITNESS: Yes, yes, it was.

LAWYER: Is it also your contention that there is an abundance of written evidence to support your treatment?

WITNESS: Yes, there is.

LAWYER: Is this the list of references you have quoted this afternoon to support your care? I am referring to Exhibit A, part 2.

WITNESS: Yes.

LAWYER: And you say there are more where these came from?

WITNESS: Yes.

LAWYER: I have nothing more at this time. I believe
the doctor has made his position clear and I will discuss with my client whether or not we should pursue
this action further.

Then the doctor awoke and realized it was all a dream. Cases are not
won or lost at the time of deposition and only by the grace of a summary
judgment or a favorable jury verdict may the defendant find himself free.
The deposition is not to be used alone to prove the case. It is, however, a
vital piece of evidence to be used later at the settlement table or in the
courtroom. We can go so far as to say that the pre-trial depositions are
probably the most powerful pieces of evidence because they represent
carved-in-stone testimony of all the parties involved. They serve as a record
for the court should any witness be absent from the trial, and they can be
used as tools for impeachment of trial testimony.

The Mutual Insurance Company of Arizona (MICA) writes in its handbook for the physician defendant:

"Your deposition can be an unsettling experience...
But if you are persuaded that you treated the plaintiff
to the best of your ability — that your treatment complied with the standard of care — then you can expect
to perform well in your deposition."

It would be easy for a physician to assume that since he did the right
thing and has hard evidence to back it up, a question and answer session
with the plaintiff's lawyer would be a walk in the park. Nothing could be
further from the truth. A doctor might have performed admirably in a clinical
situation and yet he could easily be manipulated by a sly attorney into
wording his answers in such a way as to strengthen the case for the other
side.

My very first deposition was given for a malpractice case against my
training hospital in California. The patient's attorney began by telling me:

"A deposition ...is a court-authorized proceeding.
...you have been placed under oath, and all of my
questions and all of your answers are being taken
down by the reporter.

If I ask a question which is unclear, or ...you feel we
are failing to communicate, I want you to stop and
ask me to ask the question in a fashion that you can
understand...

> And this is an oral experience. We have to speak out.
> A shake of the head, a shrug of the shoulders, un-huh,
> and huh-uh are just real hard on the reporter. ...answer
> out loud, use yes or no..."

If I were a lawyer giving an unsuspecting witness instructions, I would probably say something like this.

> "A deposition is a court-authorized proceeding. You
> are under oath, but I am not. There is no judge here to
> control the conduct of the participants. You may confer
> with your attorney at any time.
>
> I will take whatever steps are necessary to get you to
> answer questions in such a way as to support my cli-
> ent's position. You would be wise not to volunteer any
> information."

A deposition is not just a record for the court. It is an opportunity for the plaintiff's counsel to gain a world of information about the defendant. It is also the first chance (hopefully, the only chance) the lawyer has to see how easy it will be to convert the defendant into the plaintiff's best witness.

The main objectives

I have identified three goals I believe lawyers will attempt to achieve: estab-lish inappropriate delays, turn debatable issues into facts, and spread the blame. Each has the potential to create support for the plaintiff's contention that a physician, nurse, hospital, et al. deviated from care that would be considered reasonable and ordinary. We will see how successful completion of one or more of these goals can strengthen the plaintiff's case.

Establishing delays

Plaintiffs' lawyers are big on delays: delays in diagnosis, delays in treatment, delays in response to critical situations. A time frame that seems routine to us can be presented to a jury as inordinately long. We have already seen in Chapter 7 how a witness can be pressured into giving testimony that is not only inaccurate but supportive of the plaintiff's position. It would stand to reason that a physician, nurse, or other hospital staff demonstrating a delay in one area could sway a jury into assuming that there were similar delays leading to breaches of care standards in other areas of the patient's management.

The following is from a deposition in a malpractice case. Here the ques-tioning centers around the time needed to get a report on an arterial blood gas sample.

> LAWYER: Will it be your testimony, Dr. Brown, that it probably took longer than one to two minutes from the time the sample was drawn until the results were called into the operating room?
>
> WITNESS: From the time the arterial blood gas is drawn until you have a report verbally over the phone, yes, it takes more than a minute.
>
> LAWYER: Does it take more than two minutes?
>
> WITNESS: It's been my experience that it takes more than two minutes.
>
> LAWYER: Under emergency stat circumstances such as existed in this case, it is your testimony that it probably took longer than two minutes?
>
> WITNESS: For the entire process to take place, yes.
>
> LAWYER: How long, Dr. Brown?
>
> WITNESS: I don't know.
>
> LAWYER: Can you give me any estimate at all?
>
> WITNESS: No.
>
> LAWYER: Just that it was more than two minutes?
>
> WITNESS: It was more than two minutes.

From the time the sample is taken to the nearest blood gas analyzer until the results are called will probably take more than two minutes unless the machine is at the patient's bedside. The lawyer was trying to create an unprecedented delay where none existed. When asked for an estimate, the witness refused to give even an educated guess because he wanted the testimony to be as accurate as possible.

In the next example, a physician is being asked how much time elapsed between events.

> WITNESS: I do not know the exact amount of time elapsed. As an estimate, anywhere from I would say two, three, four minutes.
>
> LAWYER: As much as four minutes may have gone by?
>
> WITNESS: I would say two to four minutes.

Whether or not four minutes is an inordinate amount of time is not the issue here. It can be presented to the jury as an eternity. By the way the lawyer worded his last question, I can picture what he plans to present to the jury: "Ladies and Gentlemen of the jury, the doctor has admitted that four minutes elapsed. I ask you now to look at your watches and wait for four minutes to pass."

Turning debatable issues into facts

Even though the plaintiff's counsel will have studied the medical issues and doled out large sums of money for expert testimony, he will attempt to gain support for that testimony by eliciting the same information from other witnesses. The more testimony the plaintiff has supporting a questionable standard of care, the easier it is to convince the jury that the standard was violated. In the following example, the lawyer is trying to make the witness establish as fact the existence of a particular disease entity.

> LAWYER: In 1986, as the year went on, the diagnosis was made of Dermatomyositis in Michele's case, is that correct?
>
> WITNESS: Suspected.
>
> LAWYER: Was it just suspected by the time you had finished with her or had it been confirmed by that time?
>
> WITNESS: Let me look at the note from the internist, sir. The last admission while she was still my patient was September 23rd and it says assessment, possibility of Dermatomyositis. It doesn't say that is the diagnosis.
>
> LAWYER: Are you aware that after Michele left your care, that the diagnosis was in fact made?
>
> WITNESS: No, I am not aware.

If the lawyer could have led the witness to testify the patient had Dermatomyositis, this would have added fuel to the plaintiff's complaint. This astute doctor was also wise in reviewing her own documentation before answering the question. In her preparation for this deposition, she studied the records thoroughly and knew exactly where *to go for the information (see Chapter seven, Preparing for the deposition)*. Another example:

> LAWYER: Did you ever form an opinion that you expressed to anyone that Mary suffered from cerebral hypoxia?

WITNESS: No.

LAWYER: Have you, since the events of that day, been advised that Mary was diagnosed as suffering from cerebral hypoxia?

WITNESS: No.

LAWYER: Are you possessed of any facts that would suggest to you that that diagnosis is not true?

WITNESS: I know nothing of the diagnosis.

LAWYER: I want you to assume it to be true, that subsequent to the events of February 28th 1993, Mary was diagnosed with cerebral hypoxia. Do you have any information that would suggest that was not an accurate diagnosis for Mary?

WITNESS: May I ask a question?

LAWYER: Surely.

WITNESS: Are you stating something as fact, or are you asking me to assume something about which I know nothing?

LAWYER: I am asking you. I don't know whether you know nothing about it, and I am going to ask you some questions to find out what you do know. I do believe that you do know something about Mary. I do believe that you have spoken to several people about Mary, and I am going to ask you questions about that day. I am entitled to know what you do know. I am entitled to know what opinions you have formed and expressed to others, and I am going to ask you about those opinions today. I am going to ask you who you spoke to. I am going to ask you what you remember.

Right now, I am telling you that there was a diagnosis in Mary's medical records subsequent to February 28th 1993 that states as follows: cerebral hypoxia. Do you have any factual information that would suggest that that diagnosis, which I am asking you to assume is in her subsequent medical records, is inaccurate?

WITNESS: No, I do not.

> LAWYER: Do you know from the events that you participated in on February 28th 1993, whether or not Mary suffered cerebral hypoxia on that date?

> WITNESS: No.

The lawyer wanted the witness to support the diagnosis of cerebral hypoxia and when the witness questioned his motive, he became very irate and impatient. If the witness had accepted the diagnosis as presented, the lawyer could then focus his line of questioning on cerebral hypoxia and possibly establish support for his plaintiff's claim of cause and effect. The witness had been given no information about the cerebral hypoxia except what the lawyer was telling him at that moment, and he answered the questions accurately.

In another part of that same deposition, a question came up regarding an event involving the patient, but it was only witnessed by a relative at bedside. The plaintiff counsel's goal here was to document testimony under oath that the event occurred.

> LAWYER: Do you believe that the information should have been communicated to Dr. Jones?

> WITNESS: It might have been communicated to him if he was present at that particular time.

> LAWYER: If he wasn't present at that particular time, do you believe that the mother should have told Dr. Jones?

> WITNESS: I believe any kind of medical information from a mother or patient as it relates to their well-being is important for physicians to know.

> LAWYER: If the nurse had specifically been asked to attend the patient after that incident occurred and had evaluated the patient and had been made fully aware of all those circumstances, should that information have been communicated to the attending physicians, either by the nurse verbally or written into the chart?

> WITNESS: I am not that familiar with what is considered the standard of care for nursing documentation.

The incident in question was never reported to the nurse by the mother at the patient's bedside. The lawyer had the choice of dropping the whole issue of the incident if there was support that the nurse was never informed by the relative, or the lawyer could try to manipulate the witness's testimony to support a scenario that the nurse was aware of the incident and failed to either document it or report it directly to the physician. The event took place before the witness had any contact with the patient, but testimony could have been used to show that the nursing staff at the hospital was remiss in handling the event appropriately.

Spreading the blame

Lawyers, especially those defending other caregivers, will attempt to transfer responsibility for the patient's displeasure. In many instances, defense counsel may convince a jury that the patient himself contributed either in part or totally. Those attorneys defending the hospital and other doctors will want the jury to understand that if malpractice was involved, it was not due to impropriety on the part of their clients (see Chapter three, *The standard of care*).

Lawyers focus not so much on directly transferring the blame to someone else but more on actively stripping it away from their clients (remember *The Code of the Sinking Ship*). Like a snake losing its dead scales, the defense counsel will breathe a sigh of relief whenever testimony is given that benefits his client. Sometimes this can take a seemingly innocent form at deposition.

> LAWYER: Doctor, my name is Dudley Scratch and I represent Dr. Jones in this litigation. I understand from your testimony earlier this morning that Dr. Jones performed surgery on you, is that correct?
>
> WITNESS: Correct.
>
> LAWYER: You chose him as your surgeon?
>
> WITNESS: Yes.
>
> LAWYER: Was that procedure done under general anesthesia?
>
> WITNESS: Yes.
>
> LAWYER: So, you were asleep?
>
> WITNESS: Yes.

The witness has just given the lawyer's client a big boost — he has given testimony supporting Dr. Jones' competency because he chose him as his own surgeon, and he allowed the surgery to be performed under general anesthesia. Since Dr. Jones' management of a patient under general anesthesia was in question by the plaintiff, our witness, who is far more knowledgeable about medical matters than most jurors, just provided more credibility to Dr. Jones' position that he routinely upholds the standard of care.

Many times the questioning takes a more subtle form. In the following example, a pharmaceutical company is trying to attribute a patient's complaints to something other than its product.

> LAWYER: Did you or anyone else do a work-up for Scleroderma in Elaine's case before December of '89?
>
> WITNESS: May I look at the chart? I have told you before that Dr. Green was mainly the primary doctor at the time.
>
> LAWYER: I want to make sure you understand my question. The question is did you or anyone else do a work-up for Scleroderma before December of '89?
>
> WITNESS: I would have to look at the notes. Not that I recall.

Here it would be advantageous for the company to shift the blame for the patient's symptoms to a disease synchronous with the timing of the company's medication. Again, the physician is careful to check documentation and answer accurately.

The goal of the inquisitor to implicate others in the case can be demonstrated in the following.

> LAWYER: Who did you perceive to be the physician in charge of conducting the code?

This type of question is truly a double-edged sword. Whomever the witness names, even himself, will immediately have new responsibility placed on him and new standard of care issues to defend. The plaintiff's lawyer depends upon the infectious nature of the lawsuit to gain access to as many deep pockets as possible, and each defense counsel will attempt to protect his client from contamination.

Common forms of interrogation

If you were a witness to an event or your name appears anywhere on the chart, I cannot stress enough the importance of studying the records even if you are not named as a defendant in the lawsuit (see Chapter seven, *Preparing for the deposition*). Depending on the laws in your state, complaints may be amended later to add your name. Even if you are never named as a defendant, your testimony will be used as evidence at trial or the settlement conferences for those who have been. Anything you say during the deposition can be held against the other witnesses.

Advice from defense counsel frequently includes instructions along the lines of "Take your time, listen to the question carefully, and answer truthfully." Once in a while a shrewd lawyer will actually ask during deposition, "Has anyone told you how to answer my questions?" A straightforward response such as, "Yes, my lawyer told me to listen carefully and tell the truth," usually suffices.

The doctor may even be asked the content of any discussions he had with counsel. Before answering such questions, the witness should look to counsel for advice since the conversations may be privileged and, therefore, not discoverable. Hopefully, the lawyer for a defendant will speak up and object to the question as well as instruct the witness not to answer. My all-time favorite response follows.

> LAWYER: Did you meet with anyone before today's deposition to discuss your proposed testimony?
>
> WITNESS: I met with Mr. Smith for five or ten minutes.
>
> LAWYER: When was that, sir?
>
> WITNESS: At 8:15 to approximately 8:25 or 8:30.
>
> LAWYER: Capture the substance of that conversation, if you would, please.
>
> WITNESS: He said there was an attorney coming from Phoenix who doesn't do much but try to irritate doctors. He said that we will be represented, I believe the phrase he used was hillbillies, bumpkins out in the sticks who didn't care about patients. He just kind of warned me how you would present yourself and maybe a pointer or two on how to deal with it.

As we examine some of the common questions, we must study not only the form of the questions but the actual purpose of the line of questioning as well. A witness may be told by counsel not to worry about the reasoning behind the questions asked, just give the best answer as truthfully and accurately as possible. I hold the opinion that a witness will be less fearful of his inquisitor if he is able to determine where the lawyer is heading in the questioning, much like a kidnapped victim peeking out from under his blindfold.

This approach helps to lay groundwork for a better defense. The lawyer will appear to be seeking information when he is actually attempting to gather as much support as possible for the plaintiff's claim, real or imagined.

In the beginning

It is well known that if a frog is dropped into boiling water, the frog will hop right out of the pot. If, however, the frog is placed in cool water and that water is allowed to heat slowly to a boil, the frog will sit there and cook. Lawyers are aware that such an amphibian tendency exists in witnesses and the deposition will usually begin in a cool, harmless fashion.

Most depositions begin with benign questions designed to give the lawyer an idea of your composure and your responsiveness. A set of interrogatories was, more than likely, completed prior to your deposition, so the lawyer will know where you live, where you work, and your basic background. Once in a while, however, a lawyer may not waste any time getting to the meat of the matter as demonstrated by this initial question asked of a doctor defendant immediately after he was sworn in.

> LAWYER: Dr. Jones, tell us every factual basis for your claim that Dr. Smith was negligent and caused Martha's brain damage?

Following are examples of the more commonly asked questions in the beginning of the deposition.

- Will you state your name, please?
- You are a medical doctor?
- Where are you presently residing?
- Have you ever had your deposition taken before? Can you tell me how many times?
- Can you give me a brief outline of your educational background and your training and experience?

In the following example, we can imagine how the witness appeared to the inquisitor even though the question seems harmless.

> LAWYER: Would you state your name for the record, please?
>
> WITNESS: Nancy Nurse.
>
> LAWYER: You can relax, we don't bite. We are all late, but we'll plunge right on here and see how far we can get.

The witness obviously appeared nervous. This example might be better placed under *Untruths and False Assumptions* since the lawyer is clearly understating his intentions (*we don't bite*).

The plaintiff's attorney may want to examine your style before attacking the main issues, or he may want to ruffle your feathers at the onset. In either event, be prepared.

Begging the question

This form of questioning can be traced back to the 16th century. It allows the inquisitor to stack the deck, so to speak, in his favor before the actual oral confrontation begins. The lawyer is essentially *begging* for an argument, but the modern-day use of this technique is to establish as fact something which has never been proven. The most famous example: "When did you stop beating your wife?".

The attorney will ask a question in such a way as to get verification from the witness of a situation which may or may not actually exist. It is probably one of the most dangerous forms of questioning and, naturally, one of the most popular. The witness must be alert to this tactic and listen carefully to each word in any given question. My favorite example comes from *The Holy Bible* (Luke 10:25):

> "And, behold, a certain lawyer stood up, and tempted
> him, saying, Master, what shall I do to inherit eternal
> life?"

A person need do nothing to be a beneficiary. I have always held the opinion that by wording his question in this manner, the lawyer wanted Jesus to confirm his claim that eternal life was a right by birth. Note the following example from a deposition.

> LAWYER: How quickly after the events took place on
> October 13, 1990 did you become aware that there was
> a controversy?

> WITNESS: Probably very rapidly after.

The key word in the lawyer's questioning is *controversy*. The witness, by answering the question under oath, is establishing a fact that controversy existed. Speaking with the witness after the deposition, she explained that she misunderstood and thought the lawyer was asking about any conversation that took place after the event in question. Her misunderstanding established a fact in the case that had not existed before: there was controversy over the event. Later in the same deposition.

> LAWYER: You told me when we started this deposition that the matter became somewhat controversial after the events of that day. When did you first recognize that it was an item of discussion at the hospital?

Upon review of the entire deposition, our witness did not tell the lawyer the matter became controversial, but she affirmed his earlier statement, and in doing so, established a situation that could be viewed as fact by the judge and jury even though a controversy may or may not have existed. In another example, a physician witness is being questioned.

> LAWYER: Other than this case, were there any other cases down in Anytown where you expressed your displeasure about some of the care rendered by Dr. Jones, Smith or Brown?

Upon review of the deposition, the doctor did not express any displeasure about this case, but the lawyer would have liked to establish as fact that he did. This would support the plaintiff's contention that there had been a deviation from the standard of care.

Defense counsel will often advise witnesses to answer the questions and refrain from trying to analyze them. I believe the witness would be wise to consider what it is the lawyer is attempting to prove. Our inquisitor may not be so interested in the answer as he is in the verification of an issue hidden within the question.

In the following example, the lawyer is trying to transfer some of the blame to a witness who was not named as a defendant in the case.

> LAWYER: Have you, Dr. Jones, ever been in charge of a resuscitation of a patient who coded on the table before this?

> WITNESS: I have been involved in cardiac arrest on the operating table.

> LAWYER: To the best of your recollection, prior to May 1st, 1983 had you ever been in charge of a patient who coded on the table during surgery?

> WITNESS: The problem I am having with your question is I do not understand what you mean by in charge.

It is clear the lawyer wanted a *yes* or *no* answer to establish as fact that Dr. Jones had been *in charge* of this particular resuscitation.

A couple of things can be learned from the above answers. For one, the initial answer to the question should have been worded differently. It is almost as if the witness was thinking out loud (see Chapter ten, *Traps to avoid*). The witness, however, quickly realized the possible implication of her response. The question that followed was easier to answer.

> LAWYER: Have you ever been involved with a surgery, let's make it a pediatric patient, where the patient coded on the table while under anesthesia before May 1st, 1983?
>
> WITNESS: No.

The key word in this question is *pediatric*. She had admitted previously that she had been involved in resuscitations in the operating room, but those patients were all adults. The lawyer unknowingly narrowed the field. The answer to part of his question was *no*, so the whole answer was *no* (see Chapter ten, *Traps to avoid*).

Hindsight is always 20/20 and a better answer would have been

> LAWYER: Have you, Dr. Jones, ever been in charge of a resuscitation of a patient who coded on the table before this?
>
> WITNESS: I cannot answer your question the way it is stated.

Compound questions

Lawyers will frequently ask questions that contain more than one part. This puts a burden on the witness who has to word the answer to the first part with care while remembering the second.

This can be an open form of questioning that gives the witness a carte blanche to talk. From the answer, which can be as long as the witness desires, the lawyer may siphon hints which will allow him to divert his questioning to a related subject. A spontaneous answer to a compound question runs the risk of divulging more information than is necessary.

> LAWYER: When we use the term induction, what does that mean to you? How should we explain to a jury, this is what Dr. Smith means when he says induction?

There are clearly two separate issues here: What does *induction* mean to the witness and how should the term *induction* be explained to a lay jury? It would be appropriate for the witness to politely say, "Your question has two parts. Which part would you like me to answer first?" This tactic is used in the following example.

> LAWYER: When you respond to a call and someone's having difficulty breathing, tell me when you would use a non-rebreather mask with oxygen, when you would use a bag valve mask with a bag valve, and when you would intubate someone?
>
> WITNESS: Could we address each one individually?
>
> LAWYER: Sure.
>
> WITNESS: Which one would you like me to start with?

The lawyer usually gets the impression at this point that the witness is sensitive to compound questions and may make it a point throughout the remainder of the deposition to be more careful. As a rule of thumb, the more specific the question, the fewer words needed to answer it.

Lawyers at trial are more prone to pin the witness down with shorter, to-the-point questions. Juries do not like rambling witnesses, but lawyers love to hear the witness open up at deposition and spill enough beans to provide support for their client as well as give the lawyers ideas and direction for further questioning. *Any witness who offers more information than required is doing himself a disservice and is aiding and abetting the opposition.* Another example from a deposition:

> LAWYER: Could you give us just a little bit of a background in narrative form of your medical training and your medical experience, please?

Here the lawyer wants information about both the doctor's training and experience. The witness has the opportunity to ask for more specifics. Does the lawyer want the name of the medical school and training hospital and in what specific experience is he interested?

There is a tendency among inexperienced witnesses to babble for several minutes in answering compound questions, and this should be avoided if possible. If the doctor goes into detail about his experience, he may be offering information that the lawyer can use to show a judge or jury that his experience in a particular area is either too limited or may be sufficient enough to warrant expert status. Being declared an expert has its downside; the lawyer may try to convince the jury that the witness was experienced enough to know better.

We saw in Chapter 7 another example of a compound question.

> LAWYER: Tell me the procedure which you go through and how these entries are made. How come part of this is your handwriting and part of it is the girl's handwriting?

The witness should ask the lawyer to break down the question into specific parts. These questions can always be divided so the witness only has to concentrate on one part at a time.

Generalized questions

Also known as a free-will question, this type of interrogation invites the witness to expound *ad nauseum* within the confines of the subject matter presented. As with the compound format, the witness needs to pin down the inquisitor to specifics since this form is even more open-ended. The generalized question is usually used when the lawyer is unfamiliar with the specifics of an issue or he is running out of ammunition for further questioning. This is clear in the following example.

> LAWYER: Tell us everything you did from the time the alarms went off until the time when a pulse and blood pressure were reestablished.

The lawyer wants the witness to paint a picture of his activity surrounding the incident in question. The answer should be based on documentation and the witness's recall of events. Any sequencing errors the witness might make in answering this question could come back to haunt him later. A reasonable response might be, "There were a lot of things going on at that time. Could you please be more specific as to what you want to know?" Another scenario might be as follows.

> LAWYER: Tell us everything you did from the time the alarms went off until the time when a pulse and blood pressure were reestablished.
>
> WITNESS: I did what would be expected of me in such a situation.
>
> LAWYER: What exactly did you do?
>
> WITNESS: Which particular moment are you asking about?
>
> LAWYER: Well, let's say the very beginning. What was the first thing you did?

The witness has pinned the lawyer down to a more specific line of questioning and there is no longer the need to pull answers out of the air and risk taking events out of order. The unsuspecting witness can open the door himself to a generalized question.

> LAWYER: Do you have any factual basis for making such a claim?
>
> WITNESS: Do I personally? There are things in the record that would indicate that some things that they wished to have done, accomplished, were not accomplished.
>
> LAWYER: Tell me everything in the record that falls under the heading of those things that they wished to do that were not done.

The original question asked for a *yes* or *no* answer. The response opened a Pandora's box of new information for the lawyer to examine.

Depositions are frequently ended with generalized questions.

> LAWYER: Is there any recollection that you have concerning the events of July 17th that you have not told me about in this deposition?
>
> WITNESS: No.

This generalized question took the form of an *absolute*. The lawyer attempted to pin the witness down to carved-in-stone testimony so there would be no surprises during the trial. If the witness embellished upon the deposition testimony at trial with more details, the lawyer might impeach that testimony by showing the court that the witness had no such recall at the time of deposition. A better answer can be found in another deposition.

> LAWYER: I may have asked you something earlier but then a later question may have triggered an answer in your mind, and I want to give you time right now to tell me if there's anything that you recalled later that would change an earlier answer? If you recall anything, I'd be happy for you to tell me now.
>
> WITNESS: Unless you have something to jog my memory, I don't recall anything, no.

Here the witness has left a door open. His memory might be *jogged* at a later date. Witnesses are often coached by attorneys to respond with, "That is all I can remember at this particular time."

Untruths and false assumptions

The witness at a deposition is the only person taking the oath to tell the truth, the whole truth, and nothing but the truth. The lawyers asking the questions are not under oath. A clever attorney may attempt to milk information from an unsuspecting witness by making statements that are not founded in fact but will become fact when the witness, under oath, acknowledges them as such.

An example of a lawyer's attempted chicanery was already been alluded to in Chapter 7. Here is another.

> LAWYER: My partner took a deposition of Dr. Jones the other day and he at least gleaned an impression Dr. Jones was, for some reason, upset with you. Would you know of any reason for that?

For the record, careful examination of Dr. Jones' deposition does not reveal any testimony that could be interpreted as derogatory. In fact, the name of the above witness rarely came up. Here the lawyer is wanting the witness to offer information regarding any controversial management, and in doing so, he can strengthen his case for possible deviation from care standards. This can also serve to support *The Achilles Principle*: Find the witness's weak spot and he will crumble.

In another situation, a young physician received a subpoena to appear at a deposition. Since he was not named in the lawsuit, he immediately called the plaintiff's lawyer and asked why he was being deposed. As we know, this is not an act recommended by our liability carriers. Below is an example of why we should not have contact with the plaintiff's counsel without our attorney's permission.

> LAWYER: Mr. Smith asked that I, my secretary actually, who is far more reliable than I, fax a copy of a legal document we filed that attempted to incorporate the substance of a telephone conversation we had when you called my office. Have you had an opportunity to look at that?
>
> WITNESS: I reviewed that yesterday with Mr. Smith.
>
> LAWYER: Did you see anything in that document that struck you as erroneous, that wasn't the way you had put it?

> WITNESS: There were a few things that were, one thing that was, which was wrong, and a few things that could be construed one way or the other.

Unbeknownst to the young physician at the time of the call, the lawyer actually took notes and filed a legal document on the matter. Now the witness is faced with details of his own telephone call and has to make corrections since the lawyer no doubt wrote it to suit his own needs.

A plaintiff's lawyer may start a question with "I want you to assume it to be true" when such a remark is not supported by factual evidence. Just as I stressed the need for a witness's answers to be accurate, the information in the questions should be backed up by factual documentation. Only then can the witness feel assured that his answers reflect the truth.

Here is an example from a deposition of a lawyer's attempt at turning an assumption into fact.

> LAWYER: Assume that Dr. Jones were to testify that no one at the time knew the proper dosage to give for a pediatric patient of Mary's size, would you agree or disagree with that statement?

In the following deposition, the doctor listened very carefully to the lawyer's question.

> LAWYER: I'd like you to assume that in late 1984 or early 1985, the diagnosis of Lupus was confirmed in Maria. It was in early 1984, like in November, that you started suspecting, you or others started suspecting that she might have Lupus?
>
> WITNESS: I don't want to assume anything. I like facts.

If there had been a question of whether or not this patient had Lupus diagnosed, concurring with the lawyer's assumption would have settled the issue for the court. Witnesses must be aware of and alerted to the premise that the lawyer may not be telling the truth.

Occasionally, the untruth will be blatant. In a deposition, I was asked the following question.

> LAWYER: Now, I have been advised that there was a case against you, Yuma Regional Medical Center and several other doctors which has recently been transferred to the superior court in Maricopa County involving medical negligence. Have we covered that?
>
> WITNESS: I have no idea what you are talking about.

It would be highly unusual for a medical malpractice case against me to be tried in a Superior Court other than the one in Yuma County since that is where I reside and practice. Employing the Achilles Principle, the lawyer was hoping to startle me with that information and, therefore, divert my attention away from interrogation more germane to the subject at hand. A witness unfocused on the questions is a witness exploitable.

Leading questions

This form of interrogation can be helpful to a defendant on a witness stand during trial when the defense counsel may want the jury to have a particular piece of information that has not been delivered by the witness yet. The lawyer may begin a line of questioning with "Isn't it true...". This offers the defendant the opportunity to mention something that he either forgot or didn't perceive as important.

During a deposition the inquisitor will use this tactic to establish something as fact and, at the same time, record the witness's testimony as being in line with the plaintiff's position. In the following example, the lawyer is setting the witness up to establish a lack of communication between two physicians.

> LAWYER: Any special features of the case would require a person-to-person phone call with Dr. Jones or Smith, whoever the attending is, right?
>
> WITNESS: That is right.
>
> LAWYER: And you felt that there were no special features in this case because there was no such phone call, right?
>
> WITNESS: There was no telephone call because there was no necessity, there was no indication for that.
>
> LAWYER: So the method and manner of communication between the two offices is obviously on paper, lab report, EKG tracings, consultation reports, special information. For example, the lab tests you got after the 23rd of August, right?

Instead of asking the physician, the lawyer is spoon-feeding information into the record for the witness to confirm. Also, note the use of the adjective *special* (see Chapter ten, *Traps to avoid*). Clever counsel will convince the jury that the plaintiff was, indeed, a very *special* patient even though the treating physician felt that *there were no special features in this case.*

In the following exchange, the witness carefully avoids committing himself to the testimony offered by the lawyer.

> LAWYER: Did you mention the medication by name
> or not?
>
> WITNESS: I can't remember that.
>
> LAWYER: So you can't in good faith state you said,
> "You know, it's really important, Mrs. Gerlach, you
> better get back on your blood thinner because you
> could embolize." You didn't tell her that, did you?
>
> WITNESS: I wouldn't say I didn't tell her, I don't
> remember.

The above questioning style is more commonly seen in the courtroom.
Even though it is unusual for a seasoned malpractice lawyer to lead a witness
during the deposition testimony, a wise witness will not allow a lawyer to
establish the facts of the case by putting words in his mouth.

Distracting questions

In the beginning of the deposition, there will probably be a line of questioning concerning the doctor's place of residence, time in practice, place of
training, etc. The plaintiff's lawyer will already know the answers, but this
will afford him the chance to ascertain how responsive the witness will be.
It is also a chance for the lawyer to convince the witness that the questions
will be harmless and there is nothing to fear.

Later in the deposition, the lawyer may revert to questions of an innoc-
uous nature again. This usually occurs when the lawyer thinks he has put
the witness under a lot of pressure and beneficial answers are not coming.
The lawyer can divert his interest temporarily to give the witness a chance
to cool down and reestablish confidence in the inquisitor.

A sudden change of subject matter can also mean that the lawyer has
run out of ideas on that particular subject and needs a little time to reorganize
his thoughts. The witness will feel relieved that an uncomfortable line of
questioning is over when, in fact, he is only being offered breathing space
for the moment. This false hope may cause the witness to forget how the
previous questions were answered and accurate recollection may be difficult
when confronted with the same line of questioning again.

Hypothetical questions

Lawyers will attempt to prove a deviation from the standard of care by
showing the fact finders that in any other circumstance, the sick or injured

plaintiff would have been handled differently. A case can also be strengthened by removing any possible contribution the patient made on his own behalf.

> LAWYER: If one assumes you waited five minutes to give the drug, do you have any reason to believe that it would not have had a similar effect on Mr. Harvey three to five minutes sooner?

> WITNESS: You're making a very large assumption, that I waited five minutes before I gave it.

The lawyer wants the court to believe his patient would have had a normal response to the drug if it had been given sooner and a five-minute delay can be presented to a jury as a lifetime.

In the following example, the lawyer cleverly combines the leading technique while setting up a hypothetical situation.

> LAWYER: Could Mr. Collins' agitation also have been a reaction to hypoxia?

> WITNESS: The reaction may have been due to the inability to breathe properly.

> LAWYER: That results in panic, doesn't it?

> WITNESS: Yes.

> LAWYER: Not being able to get your breath is kind of a horrifying feeling, isn't it?

> WITNESS: Yes.

> LAWYER: And that may be a greater cause for someone to struggle than having the arms restrained, isn't that true?

> WITNESS: I agree.

The lawyer can present a case that the most probable reason this patient was struggling was because he was hypoxic, a piece of evidence needed to prove substandard care was employed.

Hypothetical questions can take a *what-if-you-had-it-to-do-over* form as exemplified in the following.

>LAWYER: Sitting back today and knowing what happened in this case, do you feel it would have made a difference if there had been an ambu mask on that ambulance and you had used it and bagged her?

>WITNESS: I would not have changed my treatment whatsoever. We treat every patient in the field as if they need the utmost of care. It would not have changed my treatment that night.

The above witness was later faced with a hypothetical question based upon someone else's deposition.

>LAWYER: I believe Sandy said that if the respirations were shallow and less than 10 per minute and the person was losing consciousness, she would use a bag valve mask. Do you agree with that?

>WITNESS: With my training, I would have to see the patient to make my own personal decision.

The lawyer has presented two issues for the witness to consider before answering. First, did Sandy really testify as reported by the lawyer? And how does the hypothetical situation relate to the real patient? The witness was careful to not commit to the use of a specific treatment in the situation given.

When faced with these questions, the witness must ask himself if he truly feels he upheld the standard of care. If he did, the treatment in a similar situation would, no doubt, be the same or similar. The witness would also be wise to remember that no two patients are exactly alike. There is as much diversity among the customers of health care as among the caregivers themselves.

Repetitive questions

I am reminded of a scene in the motion picture, *1-2-3*, in which Horst Buchholz is being interrogated by the East German police. They are successful in obtaining a signed confession from the handsome young hero by forcing him to listen to *The Itsy Bitsy Teeny Weeny Yellow Polka Dot Bikini* over and over and over again. Written to tickle our funny bones, this scene reinforces man's intolerance for the repetition of painful stimuli.

During a deposition a witness may become so uncomfortable giving only vague or incomplete answers to the same question over and over again, he may break down and inaccurately admit testimony just to get the inquisitor to stop. This kind of *confession* is usually just what the plaintiff's lawyer ordered. We mentioned earlier that lawyers will break the monotony by inserting distracting questions of a more benign nature but will eventually return to the tougher interrogation.

In the following example, the witness resisted the attempts to extract more information than he knew.

> LAWYER: You have not in any way familiarized your-self with the problems that Megan has had since February of '95?
>
> WITNESS: I have not been privileged to any information concerning her condition.
>
> LAWYER: Dr. Jones, is that any information, whether it was submitted to you in written form or verbally; you have no idea what has happened to Megan? Is that your testimony?
>
> WITNESS: I have no factual evidence to go on, no.
>
> LAWYER: Do you know, Dr. Jones, anything about what has happened to Megan since February, 1995?
>
> WITNESS: No.
>
> LAWYER: You have not been advised that she suffers a severe permanent neurological deficit?
>
> WITNESS: Yes, sir, you advised me of that.
>
> LAWYER: Prior to the time of this deposition, you did not know that?
>
> WITNESS: I had not been given any factual information regarding that.
>
> LAWYER: Dr. Jones, I really don't want to fence with words. My question is simple. Had you heard that, had you been told that, had you overheard conversations about that, did you have conversations about that, did you know anything about the severe permanent neurological injury that Megan had prior to this deposition?
>
> WITNESS: Mr. Scratch, what I am telling you is I have had no factual knowledge given to me.

Please note how the witness did not immediately take the lawyer's statement about the severe neurological injury as fact. I find it interesting that the lawyer did not want to fence with words since the study of law involves arguments over the ambiguity of words and phrases. Any witness in a deposition would be wise to remember that his first response is probably the most correct one and he should refrain from altering it unless he must do so to uphold the truth.

Looking at exhibits

It is not unusual for a plaintiff's lawyer or counsel for another defendant to present to the witness a document of some kind. It may be an affidavit, a written statement that the witness will be allowed to read and comment upon. More often than not, the exhibit will take the form of a sketch or drawing made by another witness.

If a witness answers questions based upon such a sketch or drawing, the witness is, in effect, affirming the accuracy of the exhibit. Here again, we have to call upon *The Cherry Tree Rule*: before responding to questions about such exhibits, we must be sure that they are accurate and truly reflect whatever it is they represent.

Summary

A defendant in a malpractice deposition must be aware that the opposing counsel will attempt to turn each witness for the defense into the best witness for the plaintiff. This can be done by showing the court that inappropriate delays occurred, documenting factual issues that were once debatable, and making each health care provider responsible in one way or another for the death of or injury to the patient. The witness must listen for the inquisitor's use of untruths, false assumption, compound questions, generalized questions, leading questions, hypothetical questions, and other means of interrogation meant to stack the deck in the plaintiff's favor.

References

Aron, R. and Rosner, J. L., *How to Prepare Witnesses for Trial*, McGraw-Hill Book Company, 1985.

Felleman, H. (Ed.), *The Best Loved Poems of the American People*, Doubleday, 1936.

Keeton, R. E., *Trial Tactics & Methods*, Little Brown & Company, 1973.

Kennan, D., Deposing the defendant doctor: Preparation is crucial, *Trial*, 26, 69.

Malone, D. M. and Hoffman, P. T., *The Effective Deposition*, National Institute for Trial Advocacy, 1996.

Mutual Insurance Company of Arizona, *The Physician-Defendant, A Handbook*.

Zobel, H. B. and Rous, S. N., *Doctors and The Law*, W. W. Norton & Company, 1993.

chapter ten

Traps to avoid

"Why may not that be the skull of a lawyer? Where be his quiddities now, his quillets, his cases, his tenures, and his tricks?"

William Shakespeare
(Hamlet, Act V, Scene 1)

As we mentioned in Chapter eight (*Meeting the inquisitor*), the lawyer deposing the witness will try to appear harmless and nonthreatening. He is only there to seek information. The same counsel, during a jury trial, will have a whole different demeanor. In the courtroom environment, it is to the plaintiff's advantage to demonstrate to the jurors how strongly the lawyer believes in his client. Taking a more accusatory position will strengthen the case for negligence or even malicious intent.

However, during the deposition the lawyer wants to make the witness feel comfortable, like the spider extending the hospitality of his web to the unsuspecting fly. Even if the answers are not exactly what the lawyer was hoping for, he will still maintain an even calm. If the witness studies the questions carefully and avoids implicating himself or anyone else, the attorney may begin to show frustration. Personally, I consider it a positive sign that he is failing in achieving his goals.

The skunk principle

During my surgery training in California, I had the pleasure of working with a fine senior resident who taught me a memorable lesson — *Never get into a pissin' match with a skunk*! You will not only lose, you will come away sporting a most unpleasant odor.

We can apply this Skunk Principle to the deposition. No matter how upset the inquisitor is with the witness, it is imperative that the lawyer never see any signs of aggression from across the table. The witness must maintain absolute control of his temper and responses.

Any form of defiant behavior does not, by itself, show up in the final form of the deposition, but lashing out must be seen as only coming from the plaintiff's side. It is not a matter of the witness going into lecture mode and telling the lawyer how he really feels as much as there is a risk that the witness will blurt out remarks that he may regret later.

The fact finders are not surprised to see the attorneys showing aggression and frustration during the course of the lawsuit, but it appears inappropriate for a member of the medical profession to do the same. A temper tantrum is exactly what the plaintiff's counsel would like to see to support his contention that the doctor or nurse allows emotions to interfere with judgment. After all, we are not suppose to take the lawsuit personally in the first place.

The defense witness has an important tool available: the sound of silence. Creative use of this tool may or may not defuse an angry lawyer, but it can demonstrate the ability of the witness to maintain his cool during a volatile situation. During one of my depositions, the lawyer had failed on several occasions to extract information that I considered to be within the realm of peer review and, therefore, not admissible as evidence. His frustration with me is obvious in the following exchange.

> PLAINTIFF'S LAWYER: When this deposition is over, I am not going to terminate the deposition. I am going to suspend it, because the law is clear that is not what peer review is.

> MY LAWYER: I am not going to agree to suspend it. I think you can establish whatever foundation you need to determine…

> PLAINTIFF'S LAWYER: You want to instruct the witness that her understanding of protected peer review is incorrect?

> MY LAWYER: I don't think her understanding has anything to do with the issue. She is not a lawyer or a judge. But my point is I am not going to agree to suspend the deposition.

> PLAINTIFF'S LAWYER: I don't want to belabor this deposition by getting into a fight with her or you or anyone else in this room as to what is or is not a proper definition of peer review. I don't think there is anything valid served by that.

> MY LAWYER: I am going to tell you not to ask her questions about those conversations today, and I am

also telling you that I am not going to agree to bring
her back.

It does not take much of an imagination to picture two men propping
themselves up on the table with their arms screaming at each other. I was
fortunate to have an attorney who did not allow the plaintiff's counsel to
continue with an inappropriate line of questioning. During the ranting and
raving I sat perfectly still completely dissociated from the argument. Even
though the row was about me and my answers (or lack of answers), defending myself would have served no purpose in the deposition and the recorded
words only stood to make the plaintiff's lawyer look bad.

Watch for contradictory statements

It's important to keep your guard up at all times during the deposition.
Listen carefully to each question and make sure the attorney's words in one
question do not lead you to alter an answer already given. An example:

> LAWYER: Now, that information to restart the drug
> was not in your records as of March 10th, was it?
>
> WITNESS: It was not in my record, but I did tell the
> patient to take it.

A few minutes later in the questioning:

> LAWYER: You made no order on March 10th that she
> should resume taking the pills, did you?
>
> WITNESS: No, I did not.

The doctor already told counsel that an order had been given, he just
didn't write it down. Had this case gone to trial, I guarantee that the lawyer
for the plaintiff would have delivered this latter response to the jury in
technicolor and Dolby sound.

Beware of questions asking you to elaborate

Most plaintiffs' lawyers do not have degrees in medicine and, while they
will try to educate themselves in the nuances pertaining to the case, they
still need a lot of help. A successful witness can put a lawyer in an intellectual
corner with no way out.

The lawyer, not knowing where to go from there, may ask the witness
to elaborate more on something that was just said. The clever witness will
respond: "What specific part do you want more information about?"

A good rule: Only answer specific questions. If the lawyer wants elaboration, he needs to itemize his interests and ask about them one at a time.

Analyze compound questions carefully

Here, again, it is imperative that the witness makes sure the lawyer has worded the question in such a way as to elicit a specific answer. If you are having trouble forming the answer, chances are the question is too vague, too generalized, or has more than one part. You have every right to ask the lawyer to break down the question into each part and focus on only one thing at a time.

Resist the temptation to correct the lawyer

During a deposition you are not being paid to educate. In fact, you aren't being paid at all. Your only responsibility is to answer the questions. If the lawyer asks a question using a term you don't understand or know is incorrect, then you simply cannot answer the question as stated.

It is not your place to correct the lawyer, although he will be very grateful if you do. Also, rewording a question for the lawyer will in no way assist in proving your innocence. The trial will not be won or lost at your deposition. An example:

> LAWYER: Do you have any reason to believe that this drug would not have had a similar effect on Jason's heart three to five minutes sooner?
>
> WITNESS: The question would be…
>
> DEFENSE LAWYER: No. Just a second. Can we have the question read back, please?

At this point, the witness's lawyer jumped in and prevented a blunder. It is not our job to restate or clarify questions. The inquisitor has that responsibility. In another situation,

> LAWYER: At the time of the operation, was the patient's relation exchange volume normal?
>
> WITNESS: The most noticeable abnormality was the end-tidal CO_2, which was relatively high.

The lawyer didn't ask about the end-tidal CO_2. He wanted information about a "relation exchange volume," whatever that is. I do not believe the question could have been answered the way it was stated, and the witness's response only gave the lawyer another idea to pursue — the end-tidal CO_2.

Answer a question only if you understand it

This rides in tandem with the warning mentioned above. If a question makes no sense, the witness can't answer it. It is not the witness's role to rephrase the question to make it understandable.

Guessing is out!

This is not a Board Exam. No points are given for coming up with the right answer. The correct response is simply the truth delivered with accuracy.

A favorite ploy of plaintiff lawyers is to drill the witness with questions pertaining to his particular field of knowledge and skill. An orthopedic surgeon being sued by a patient over a fractured hip complaint might be asked to explain the different types of fractures and their respective managements.

It is difficult enough to remember the contents of the medical records and the events surrounding the case without this added stress. My only advice is to answer the questions if you can. If you are concerned that you may give an incorrect or incomplete response (which, I guarantee, will be stuffed down your throat at trial), you might simply state that you are concerned your answers may not be complete or accurate at that time and would, therefore, not reflect your usual knowledge base or the level of care you give your patients.

An alternative approach might be to ask for a break during which time you can regroup your thoughts more clearly. This would be hard to justify if the lawyer begins his questioning with this approach. An hour or so into the deposition it would be more appropriate.

As mentioned earlier, try to avoid the "estimate" trap. The lawyer may persist in extracting a definite number or time from the witness. The attempt may cover several minutes of the inquisition and the witness may blurt out an answer just to shut the lawyer up. A better approach is to ride it out. For instance,

> LAWYER: Can you give me an approximate time as somebody who participated in the events and the conversation or process that you are describing? (Note the compound question.)
>
> WITNESS: No, I can't.
>
> LAWYER: You can't give me any help at all in terms of when this first event took place?
>
> WITNESS: I do not want to venture a guess.
>
> LAWYER: I don't need a guess, Doctor, but I am entitled to your best estimate, if you can give it. I am going

to try to find some way to break down these several conversations you reported to me. I need to tag them. We can call it the first one, but I'd like to have at least a general idea. Was it within the first week as best you recall?

WITNESS: I do not recall.

The above was taken from a deposition of mine. I could not truthfully or accurately answer his question and I refused to give any estimate that I might find to be in error at a later date. The lawyer's frustration with me shone through the written word.

Watch the use of adjectives, adverbs, and negatives

Listen very carefully to how the lawyer describes a physical finding or an untoward result. Beware of words such as "minimal" or "largest," "excruciating" or "painless." Such descriptions can be used later to decorate your testimony at trial.

Most members of the medical profession and the allied health fields are already wary of terms such as "unfortunately" and "always." Once again, listen carefully to see if the lawyer has peppered the question with even a simple word such as "never."

Likewise, try to construct your answers so as to avoid the same adjectives and adverbs. Words like "inadvertent," "unavoidable," "iatrogenic" are not helpful to your credibility at any time.

It is also a good idea to avoid negatives. Notice how the subject headings in this chapter are worded positively. There are no headings that tell you what not to do. Negatives only exist in language, not in actual experience. The linguistic negative cannot be processed by our subconscious and it will simply be discarded, much the way a teenager tunes out information he does not wish to hear.

If at all possible, construct your answers into a positive mode. People do not like hearing negative things. An example of a good exercise follows.

(Negative) "I didn't tell the nurse to discontinue the IV."
(Positive) "I told the nurse the patient might be able to have his IV removed if he could take liquids."

(Negative) "I would never tell a patient..."
(Positive) "It is my practice to tell a patient..."

(Negative) "The standard of care is not to operate right away."
(Positive) "The standard of care is to try conservative measures before surgery."

> (Negative) "Our OR is not set up for open-heart procedures."
> (Positive) "Our OR is set up for the procedures done in our community."
>
> (Negative) "No, I didn't order that blood test at that time."
> (Positive) "I ordered the blood tests I thought were appropriate for the patient's condition at that time."

Juries want to see physicians and other medical personnel in a positive light, so there is little advantage to negativism.

Resist being limited to "yes" or "no"

Even though a question is phrased to elicit a straight affirmative or negative response, it often makes us uncomfortable to do so without an opportunity to explain. More often than not, the explanation is not what the lawyer is seeking. He only wants to commit you to the answer and the answer to the record.

Let's take a hypothetical situation. We'll pretend I am being sued for a common duct injury during a laparoscopic cholecystectomy.

> LAWYER: You admit then, Dr. Uribe, that you injured the patient's common duct during the procedure?
>
> WITNESS: Yes.
>
> LAWYER: Have you been involved in cases of common duct injuries before or since this case?
>
> WITNESS: Yes.

Okay, I can dig my hole now. The lawyer will present to the jury that this was not my first common duct injury and it wasn't my last! I would expect my defense counsel to object to the insinuation, but that may or may not happen. A better response might be.

> LAWYER: Have you been involved in cases of common duct injuries before or since this case?
>
> WITNESS: I have assisted other surgeons over the years in repairing them.

Using this technique I can answer the question affirmatively and clarify what might be a sticky situation later.

Keep your thoughts to yourself

One common trait medical people, especially doctors, have is thinking out loud. We are so used to discussing clinical situations in "green light" sessions with our colleagues that it comes naturally to many of us. During a deposition it makes us look nervous and insecure about the case in question. An example:

> LAWYER: Have you changed the way you do things in your office because of this case?
>
> WITNESS: Let me think about whether or not I have changed anything. I am just talking to myself at this point.
>
> LAWYER: Do it quietly.

The plaintiff's lawyer gave this witness excellent advice. In another example:

> LAWYER: How many specialists were in town then?
>
> WITNESS: Oh, gosh. No other; let's see, one other group of, I don't know whether there was one or two specialists at that time. Doctor Jones was in town, and Doctor Smith added another specialist about that time, maybe a little bit later, I am not sure, and there was a couple of other soloists in town, Doctor Brown and Doctor Black, and I think that's all.

This witness's testimony would have been served better had he listened carefully to the question, decided on an accurate answer and replied, "I don't know how many specialists were in town then."

Listen for accuracy in the entire question

If any part of a question is wrong, the whole question is wrong. Be very careful to listen to the entire question carefully before answering. Again, please avoid the temptation to reword the question to make it easier for you to answer. Let's analyze a few possibly *inaccurate* questions.

"Did Dr. Jones speak to you that evening about Mrs. Brown's headache?" (You may have spoken with Dr. Jones that evening about Mrs. Brown, but her headache was not discussed.) The answer is "No."

"When you saw the patient in your office the following morning, didn't she mention her bleeding to you?" (You saw the patient the following day, but it was in the afternoon, not the morning.) The answer is "No."

"It is your opinion then, Doctor, that the patient's death was caused by a fat embolism?" (You made a generalized statement earlier that the patient's death was due to a pulmonary embolus.) The answer is "No."

"Is it correct, then, to say that the anesthesiologist told you a room was ready at that time?" (You were told by one of the staff anesthesiologists a room could be made available if needed.) The answer is "No."

Answer each question only once

Be very cautious about answering a question if you believe it may have a conflicting effect on an answer given earlier in the deposition. If the inquisitor returns to a previous subject an hour or so later, watch for the same line of questioning again. It is not a problem with truthfulness as it is with accuracy. Ideally, we want the record to show a correct answer, not an answer that is contradicted or altered later.

During a hearing, an attorney was interested in the questions I ask physicians when I consult on peer review matters. The conversation went something like this:

LAWYER: Exactly what questions do you usually ask?

WITNESS: I believe I answered that question earlier. My answer should be on the record.

LAWYER: Yes, but I forgot. Could you go over them again?

WITNESS: Perhaps you should try Ginko.

This was not a malpractice deposition, but I was still concerned with losing credibility if my two answers varied in any way. Had I been a defendant here I would not have made the remark about the Ginko, but I would not have succumbed to his question no matter how he badgered me. I would have also been on guard for a later question that he might slip into the proceedings to bring out the old information again.

Prepare for anything embarrassing

We know that the inquisitor will be searching for our weak spot (The Achilles Principle), and it behooves the witness to realize that any skeletons in the closet may be fair game. If you are going through a divorce at the time of the deposition, questions about your marital status may arouse anger or if your spouse recently died, any probing into your personal life will be painful. It is crucial to your performance that you maintain your composure during these sensitive moments and fend off any emotions that may interfere with your concentration.

The attorney will also search for discrepancies in our record keeping. Even though we have a tendency in everyday life to write in a hurry, it is imperative that the deposition record reflect accuracy. Notice how such an "error" on the part of the witness can be explained in this imaginary example:

> LAWYER: Would you please look at the laboratory record for June 6th?
>
> WITNESS: Yes, I see it.
>
> LAWYER: What is the patient's hemoglobin value on that date?
>
> WITNESS: It says 11.6, 11.6 grams.
>
> LAWYER: Would you now turn to your progress note dated June 6th? What is the hemoglobin value you notated here?
>
> WITNESS: It says hemoglobin 10.
>
> LAWYER: But the hemoglobin value on that day was 11.6, is that correct?
>
> WITNESS: Yes.
>
> LAWYER: Is there another test result that reports the hemoglobin to be anything other than 11.6?
>
> WITNESS: Not that I know of.
>
> LAWYER: Then, Doctor, please explain why you wrote 10 when the true result was 11.6?
>
> WITNESS: At the time my concern was whether or not the patient had a hemoglobin of 10 or higher. I simply left out the greater-than sign.

The doctor gave a plausible explanation for the variance. Doing so has made it more difficult, although not impossible, for the lawyer to present this to a jury as if the entry were in error. Note the contrast between this and the following interchange.

> LAWYER: How in the world did you end up answering your first set of interrogatories saying that you were single and unmarried?
>
> WITNESS: Unfortunately, I was somewhat pressured to sign them so that they could get them to the participating parties on time and unfortunately (there's that word again!) they were incorrect.
>
> LAWYER: You were married at that time?
>
> WITNESS: Yes, I was.

Perhaps he was only married a short time when the suit was filed, or perhaps he was single when the incident in question occurred. Whatever the reason, the witness can be presented to the jury as careless. In the following example, the witness is not shaken by the lawyer's microscopic probing.

> LAWYER: I'm going to go down to the "level". There's a number that looks like — it's hard to tell what it is. Can you explain to me what that is, that "level" number?
>
> WITNESS: The number that has been written over is a three with a number four. A level three would mean that it would be an advanced life-support skilled person providing basic life-support skills. In this case, for whatever reason, I wrote in a level of three and, of course, I intubated the patient and that was an ALS skill, so I wrote in four over the top of it.

The witness shows no sign of surprise nor does he hedge at his explanation. He wrote 3, changed his mind, and wrote 4 over it. We are told the importance of putting a single line through our documentation errors and adding our initials and date. Even though this did not occur in the above instance, the witness was ready to defend his action.

If a witness forgets whether or not he is married, or why he made a change in the documentation, perhaps he also forgot the standard of care. Preparation isn't just the key — it's everything!

Exude the right amount of confidence

A defendant who has studied and memorized everything might walk into the deposition with the attitude of "Hit me with your best shot." A word of warning — Remember *Opening Night* and the *15% Rule*. You will probably falter somehow during the ordeal. The surest way to guarantee the lawyer will find your Achilles heel early is to be overly confident.

Excessive humility doesn't work either. I would avoid playing any psychological games with the lawyer because he is going to be better at it than you are. Be yourself, but be prepared.

Summary

Any form of aggressive behavior is inappropriate during a deposition. If the inquisitor takes on an insolent or assertive approach, it is best to remember *The Skunk Principle*.

The witness should be on the look-out for questions that contain contradictory statements or ask for more elaboration. Resisting the temptation to correct a question that sounds odd or contains inaccurate information is paramount. A cautious witness will never guess at an answer nor will he be lured into limiting an answer to *yes* or *no*.

Listening carefully to the questions will help the witness pick out inaccuracies, inappropriate adjectives, and recognize multiple components. Thorough preparation before the deposition is crucial in explaining any discrepancies in the documentation. A prepared, confident witness will be a successful witness.

References

Babitsky, S. and Mangraviti, J. J., *How to Excel During Depositions: Techniques for Experts That Work*, SEAK, Inc., 1999.

Keeton, R. E., *Trial Tactics & Methods*, Little Brown & Company, 1973.

Malone, D. M. and Hoffman, P. T., *The Effective Deposition*, National Institute For Trial Advocacy, 1996.

chapter eleven

General advice

"If you need to be vague, be sure you're definite about it!"

C. Uribe, M.D.

As a first-year medical student, I recall plowing through the embryology textbook wondering by what miracle a *normal* human being can enter this world. The number and the intricacies of the steps necessary are not beyond our comprehension, but the fact that so many variables are so well orchestrated as to, more likely than not, ensure success boggles my mind.

On a lesser philosophical note, we can study the steps involved in a successful organ transplant. First, we must take into consideration the underlying medical condition of the donor; then comes the harvest and the proper handling of the organ. Concomitantly, steps are taken to ready the recipient. During the operation, the organ undergoes further preparation and the recipient is carefully monitored. If a perfusion pump is required, that will add another variable into the equation. Then comes the arduous task of keeping the new organ alive and happy in its new home. An error or *slip* at any point can mean disaster for the entire project. The same holds for malpractice depositions.

The witness entering a room to give a deposition must understand that he is only contributing a part to the whole picture, but that part can assist in building a solid defense or it can function as the weak link in the chain. Whether or not the witness is actually named as a defendant in no way diminishes the importance of his testimony.

To ensure a successful deposition, the witness must be prepared and armed with the mechanisms necessary to fend off the subterfuge the plaintiff may choose to use. I sincerely hope this book has impressed upon the reader the probability, not possibility, that this will happen. A review of the more mundane instructions given to the witness is appropriate at this point.

Answer truthfully

Perjury is still a serious matter for the common man. A defendant may have acted heroically in a given situation, but any discovered fabrication or attempted deception will only work against him in a court of law. When a witness sacrifices the truth, he sacrifices his credibility.

Maintain a neutral attitude

The witness is present at the deposition as another source of evidence in the case. He is there to answer questions and it is not his job to accuse or defend anyone. Those tasks fall under the lawyers' job descriptions.

If a witness is a defendant who feels that he upheld the standard of care, his answers will reflect that, provided he is adequately prepared. Other witnesses may have gut feelings about the case, but responding truthfully and accurately to the inquisitor should bring out the details necessary to clarify whether or not there was a breach of duty on the part of the defendants.

The inquisitor is already aware of any personal abhorrence the witness might have for him. It is not necessary to demonstrate this by glaring at the attorney or delivering answers in a caustic manner. Likewise, a seasoned inquisitor will not be swayed away from his original purpose by anything you say during the deposition. Any antagonistic questions asked by the lawyer should be answered in the same tone of voice used to give your name and address. The witness who maintains an even calm during the inquisition is a far bigger threat to the plaintiff's side than the one with a short fuse.

Listen for objections

Throughout the deposition the witness's lawyer as well as other defense lawyers in the room will call out "Objection!" This will be followed by a comment such as "Foundation," or "Form," or a more detailed explanation. It is imperative that the witness allow these objections to be recorded by the reporter. No judge is present to rule on them during the deposition, but a judge can read the objections later and decide whether or not the inquisitor's line of questioning should be discarded.

Give the lawyers a chance to object to each and every question asked. Also, it is good practice to listen when an objection is made since it may be a clue that the lawyer has asked a trick question.

Just answer the question

Deliberately withholding information is as serious as offering an answer that is false or inaccurate. In the example below, the lawyer is delving into the area of peer review.

> LAWYER: As a result of this incident, was there any investigation into your role in it?
>
> WITNESS: Not that I'm aware of.

> LAWYER: Did you receive any written reprimand, discipline, anything as a result of this incident involving Mrs. Browdy on June 29th, 1990?

> WITNESS: Not a written reprimand. I did receive a verbal commendation.

The lawyer asked if he had received *anything* as a result of the incident and the witness answered the question. Instead of simply answering *no*, the witness chose to turn a neutral situation into a supportive piece of evidence.

Listen carefully to the question

It is my policy to repeat the question to myself before giving the answer. This should only take about five seconds, provided the lawyer isn't too wordy, because inordinate delays in answering may be noted on the final transcript by the court reporter. Waiting a moment also allows the witness's counsel to object, and that objection could be a warning that a trap lies within the question. Please note how a quick response is recorded in the following deposition.

> LAWYER: Is it fair to say, then, that you do not consider yourself qualified to place a central line?

> WITNESS: Yes.

> WITNESS' LAWYER: Objection, go ahead.

> WITNESS: Yes, I do not consider myself properly trained to place a central line.

It is not uncommon to hear a question that sounds odd because the lawyer is exposing his ignorance of medicine. The witness should be careful answering a simple *no* to a question fraught with error since doing so may affirm the question as being accurate. The following example illustrates this.

> LAWYER: Did you see or note any fluid in the lungs during the intubation?

> WITNESS: Intubation does not allow you to see into the lungs.

The witness should listen carefully for untruths, contradictions, hypotheticals, repetitions, etc. At the same time, the wise witness will decide where in his mental data bank or in the documentation the answer can be found.

Answer only the question asked

It is the lawyer's job to collect the evidence and a deposition can be compared to a game of *20 Questions* although a better title might be *Four Hours Worth*. A witness who believes he is being helpful may only find himself in a more unpleasant position by handing the lawyer information about which the attorney previously knew nothing.

Any questions which seem unclear or confusing should not be altered by the witness. If you don't understand the question, simply say so. The burden during a deposition is on the lawyer to use the appropriate words and phrases to elicit the responses. It is not the job of the witness to choreograph the questions or answers to fit what the witness believes is the information the lawyer is seeking.

In the following example, the witness answered truthfully but obviously did not listen to the content of the question.

> LAWYER: Are you the one who shut off the alarms?
>
> WITNESS: Yes.
>
> LAWYER: It was your action, then, that resulted in the loss of the data?
>
> WITNESS: Yes.

Anyone who shuts off the alarms on this particular monitoring device is responsible for loss of the alarm, not the data. The machine is programmed so as to stop recording data when the alarms are off. The witness assumed a responsibility unnecessarily.

Refrain from memorizing your testimony

No script will be available to study ahead of time because a deposition is not an audition — you already have the part! It is crucial to memorize as much of the *documentation* as possible (see Chapter seven, *Preparing for the deposition*), but a witness has no idea how the lawyer will word his questions. A well-prepared witness will organize his thoughts over the events in question so that his responses will appear *de novo* and unrehearsed.

Only give best recollection of facts

The events involving a patient usually take place two or more years before your date with the plaintiff's lawyer, and it is unreasonable to assume you will be able to remember every little detail. If you cannot remember something, simply say so. If a particular action probably occurred because it was part of your *routine* at the time, inform the lawyer of this when asked.

Use everyday language

A witness does himself no favor by spouting highly technical terms or peppering his testimony with abbreviations. This not only prolongs the deposition, but the lawyer will picture the witness in front of the jury and will make plans to spend the money he stands to pocket from this case.

Even though your job at the deposition is to answer the questions as succinctly as possible, any talent you may possess for teaching will come through. If you answer each question using terms the lawyer can readily understand, he will soon imagine Our Miss Brooks demonstrating the facts to the jury.

Admit lack of knowledge

THIS IS NOT A BOARD EXAM!! It is no time for the witness to expound in depth about any subject, although the lawyer would certainly appreciate it if he did. You would be wise to limit your answers to the questions asked one at a time. Points for your side will be subtracted, not given, for excessive or superfluous testimony.

Read and sign your deposition

A physician told to me that he didn't understand what went on at the end of his deposition when the plaintiff's lawyer asked about waiving signature and his lawyer agreed to this. This meant the witness would not have the benefit of reading and correcting errors in his deposition prior to trial or settlement.

My experience with court reporters has been very positive; however, they occasionally make mistakes as well. I recall a deposition of my own in which I mentioned a *Thallium stress test* and the final document read *Valium stress test*.

A witness should always read, correct, and sign his transcript. You may be limited on the types of corrections you can make, but it is vital that whatever you did say is recorded correctly. My advice would be never waive signature and never allow your lawyer to waive it for you.

Summary

No matter what the attorney asks, answer truthfully and maintain a neutral attitude at all times. Listen carefully to the questions and give only the amount of information requested. It is best to use everyday language since the use of medical terminology may give birth to more questions asking for definitions.

If you do not know the answer, simply say so. Talking around a subject or professing the amount of knowledge you do possess serves only to provide the lawyer with more ammunition for further interrogation. Remember — This is not a Board Exam!

Never waive signature on your deposition. Always read the transcribed version and discuss with your lawyer any corrections you need to make.

References

Bibitsky, S. and Mangraviti, J. J., *How to Excel During Depositions: Techniques for Experts That Work*, SEAK, Inc., 1999.

Fish, R. M., Ehrhardt, M. E., and Beckett, J. S., *Preparing for Your Deposition*, PMIC, 1994.

Keeton, R. E., *Trial Tactics & Methods*, Little Brown & Company, 1973.

Afterword

It has been my intention to keep this book interesting, but to be successful in communicating the information, I must also make it politically correct. Hence, no book of this nature would be complete without a list of helpful hints for those health care providers who deliberately want to sabotage that prosaic piece of evidence — the malpractice deposition.

Recognizing the vast majority are interested in upholding the truth and seeing that justice is preserved, it would be unsporting of me to exclude that respectable minority who dare to push the edge of the envelope. With that in mind, I offer the following tips for those who insist on going where hundreds have gone before. These suggestions will surely guarantee a huge settlement or jury verdict against the defendant.

The Top Ten Ways to Meet Your Waterloo During a Malpractice Deposition

Number 10:	Respond to every question giving only your name, title and DEA number.
Number 9:	Try to get out as soon as possible by answering all the questions quickly even if you have to interrupt the lawyer to do so.
Number 8:	Begin your testimony by offering details on how everyone else involved in the case fell below the standard of care.
Number 7:	Tell the lawyer about all the offices you have held and the vast number of publications to your credit even if you have to fudge a little.
Number 6:	Offer as much information as you can about the rumors you've heard surrounding the case.
Number 5:	Emphasize how your management of the case not only upheld the standard of care but was the only acceptable way to handle the patient.
Number 4:	Be sure to mention that the patient is stereotypical of a particular race, ethnic group, or social class.
Number 3:	Before sending your records to the plaintiff's lawyer, add additional information using the pen you recently received for your birthday.
Number 2:	During the deposition refer to the patient as the worthless, subhuman, bottom-dwelling blob of protoplasm she really is.
And Number 1:	Make sure you *document* that the patient is a worthless, subhuman, bottom-dwelling blob of protoplasm.

Good luck and may justice prevail!

Index